Blessed Are the Nones

MIXED-FAITH MARRIAGE *and*
MY SEARCH *for* SPIRITUAL COMMUNITY

STINA KIELSMEIER-COOK

An imprint of InterVarsity Press
Downers Grove, Illinois

InterVarsity Press
P.O. Box 1400, Downers Grove, IL 60515-1426
ivpress.com
email@ivpress.com

InterVarsity Press® is the book-publishing division of InterVarsity Christian Fellowship/USA®,
a movement of students and faculty active on campus at hundreds of universities, colleges,
and schools of nursing in the United States of America, and a member movement of the International
Fellowship of Evangelical Students. For information about local and regional activities, visit intervarsity.org.

All Scripture quotations, unless otherwise indicated, are taken from The Holy Bible, New International
Version®, NIV®. Copyright © 1973, 1978, 1984, 2011 by Biblica, Inc.™ Used by permission of Zondervan.
All rights reserved worldwide. www.zondervan.com. The "NIV" and "New International Version" are
trademarks registered in the United States Patent and Trademark Office by Biblica, Inc.™

While any stories in this book are true, some names and identifying information may have been
changed to protect the privacy of individuals.

Portions of chapter one appeared in slightly different form as an essay, "The Doubt that Breathes Beside You,"
published in Image, issue 91. Used by permission.

Grace Morbitzer, Saint Jane Frances de Chantal, Elisabeth Leseur, Saint Margaret Mary,
and Saint Monica portraits, used by permission.

Cover design and image composite: David Fassett
Interior design: Daniel van Loon
Images: blue marble abstract background: © anyababii / iStock / Getty Images Plus
      starry night: © Paolo74s / iStock / Getty Images Plus
      wedding rings: © mikroman6 / Moment Collection / Getty Images
      group of nuns: © Grafissimo / DigitalVision Vectors / Getty Images
      mountain against the night sky: © Phaitoon Sutunyawatchai / Moment Collection / Getty Images
      woman standing on a dock: © Westend61 / Getty Images

ISBN 978-0-8308-4827-0 (print)
ISBN 978-0-8308-5337-3 (digital)

Printed in the United States of America ♾

InterVarsity Press is committed to ecological stewardship and to the conservation of natural resources in all
our operations. This book was printed using sustainably sourced paper.

Library of Congress Cataloging-in-Publication Data
A catalog record for this book is available from the Library of Congress.

P   25 24 23 22 21 20 19 18 17 16 15 14 13 12 11 10 9 8 7 6 5 4 3 2 1

Y   37 36 35 34 33 32 31 30 29 28 27 26 25 24 23 22 21 20

For Josh

I still choose you

CONTENTS

A LETTER TO THE READER

*D*ear One:

If you have been given this book, there is a good chance someone in your life has lost their religion. Maybe you go to church alone now. Maybe you are very brave and solo parent during the fellowship hour, attempting small talk while your unsupervised kids eat too many Oreos. Perhaps people ask about your absent spouse or child or friend, and at first you make excuses: "Peter is sick. Jenny has homework. Chris is traveling." After a month of Sundays, you become blunt: "Peter is an atheist now. Jenny is exploring Buddhism. Chris is not interested in church." The church people give you a sad look. Sometimes they whisper platitudes: "Give him time," or "She'll come around. I'll be praying for her." Their eyes go soft with pity. They twist their napkins into little snakes.

If the person you married is the one whose faith changed, I am here to say you're not alone. What the church people don't tell you is that, in any marriage, the person you wed will not be the same person you wake up with in five years, nor the same person who brings you coffee in fifteen years. That, in itself, of course, is not a bad thing—you imagine your partner will pick up an interesting new hobby (kitesurfing! CrossFit!). What you don't imagine is that one day your spouse will look you dead in the eye and say, "I don't believe in God anymore." Your husband was supposed to start kickboxing, get wrinkles, lose his hair, change careers. The premarital counseling didn't warn you that *this* might be coming, that your deep, shared spiritual reservoir might be siphoned off. Or rather, that he would close off his access, fill in the well, walk away from the tradition of looking and seeking and praying and joining with all the other tired sinners who are desperate for hope.

Sometimes relationships don't survive these kinds of changes. But it is possible that the vows, even ones made in the name of the God that one of you no longer believes in, can still hold. That even if he leaves God, God won't leave him. And that even if the vows eventually do break, that God will never leave you.

So here is my promise. This book will not save your marriage or convert your loved one; it will not offer certainties or platitudes. Instead, this book will offer my experience of faith after life veered wildly off course. It will testify to a God who is good, who blesses believers and agnostics alike.

I hope it keeps you company on your journey.

Love,

Stina

1

THE FALLOUT

I was eavesdropping, of all things, when my husband's deconversion first hit me.

I was sitting on the floor of the guest bedroom in Josh's childhood home in North Carolina, straining to make out the voices filtering through the hallway—the steady, deep timbre of my father-in-law's voice and the more volatile ups and downs of my husband's as he explained that he no longer thought God was real. My father-in-law—who previously served for twenty years as a missionary in South America, who I had seen sharing the gospel with strangers in parking lots—was now trying to talk his son back into eternal life. I closed my eyes. This was really happening. My mother-in-law was out running errands, and I wondered how she would react when she heard about this conversation later—the same mother who, when I first met her, told me that Josh was set apart for God's purposes.

It was Advent—the four weeks before Christmas that mark the beginning of a new church year. Our then two-year-old daughter, Eliza, was asleep on the bed nearby. I got up and wandered out through the hallway, out of earshot of the argument in the next room, and made my way to the living room where the Christmas tree glowed under the weight of cheerful twinkly lights. I hummed a few bars of the hymn "O Come, O Come Emmanuel," then stopped.

Standing there near the Christmas tree, I remembered other trees: how, on a perfect spring day four years earlier, Josh and I had stood under maples and pledged to serve God and each other. Guests in attendance said that the clouds were doing funny things over our heads while we recited our vows. The wispy bits of cumulus were lengthening into long pillars, eventually forming the shape of a *v*. One guest said it was the Holy Spirit dove, descending over our little ceremony. It was a sign of God's presence with us.

Now I prayed bitterly in my in-laws' living room. *What was that, God? Was the Holy Spirit dove just wishful thinking? Were the wedding vows too?* Was God really there when Josh and I made that marriage covenant? And what am I supposed to do now?

My eyes went in and out of focus as I stared at the Christmas lights, considering how full of hope Josh and I had been when we first met ten years earlier.

The first time we held hands was in a prayer circle on a mission trip during spring break at our evangelical Christian college. When we started dating at age twenty, we talked about serving together overseas or doing missionary work together. We were "on fire" for Jesus. The world was abundant with possibilities, all in service to the God we both loved.

When we got pregnant unexpectedly after our first wedding anniversary, those dreams shifted. Josh was accepted to a fully funded master's program in plant pathology, and I stayed home with our baby rather than work another nonprofit job that didn't cover the cost of childcare. My days were tethered to our baby daughter Eliza's sleep schedule, trips to the park or library, and appointments at the WIC office for vouchers that made groceries on Josh's graduate stipend affordable. My friends from college were medical residents or program managers or investment bankers, while I kept my household humming. Dishes. Vacuuming. Hanging cloth diapers on a line.

Attending church became the social highlight of my week—a chance to have conversations with adults and sing hymns and pray for the world. It was something our little family of three did together, even when I became a member of our tiny Mennonite congregation and Josh did not, saying he couldn't sign the statement of faith. Some Sundays I led worship while he sat in the pew, our daughter happily occupied in the nursery.

Maybe I should have realized that Josh was gradually losing his religion during our third year of marriage. To be sure, I knew he'd chosen not to join the church, but he still showed up by my side each Sunday. I chewed at my fingernails when he started reading the Dao De Jing, figuring it was just a phase of exploration. Nothing wrong with that. But I held on to the naive belief of the young that "everything is going to be okay." Full stop. Wasn't that the gospel I was taught all those years in Sunday school, something about everything working out for the good of those who love God? Get married, have babies, and God will provide? I knew there might be hardships, such as illness or bounced checks (marriage is hard work! all the premarital books told us). When I made my vows to Josh, I knew it wasn't going to be easy, but I expected to have a partner in faith and that we would turn to God together when faced with difficult times.

But that's not how this particular story goes.

It would be easy to make this story about my husband's faith crisis, but in fact my spiritual life started changing, too, in my midtwenties. I stopped reading my Bible, though I still packed it in my overnight bag whenever I left town. The *Book of Common Prayer* developed a permanent water ring on the front cover, functioning mostly as a coaster on my nightstand. My prayer life, once a raging river, petered into occasional drips. It wasn't that I stopped believing in God. The scandalous beauty of the incarnation, the upside-down kingdom, these things still captured my imagination. I still loved God, yet my spiritual disciplines fell away.

Was it apathy? Laziness? Cynicism? Probably. But many of my college friends were in similar places. For four years we had been immersed in an evangelical environment where spirituality was spoon-fed (and sometimes force-fed) to us every day. So much importance was placed on our individual piety, on our personal relationship with God, that it seemed inevitable we would experience a spiritual drop-off after graduating, as our small, protected pool was sucked into the big, wide ocean.

As time passed, I grew afraid of examining my own beliefs. I felt like author Kathleen Norris in *The Cloister Walk*, where she describes the contemplative life as plowing up the earth within her heart. "As I take my spade in hand," she writes, "as far as I can see, great clods of earth are waiting, heavy and dark, a hopeless task."

Now, at age thirty-three, I am standing here, my spade in hand, assessing my own barren fields. I am afraid of digging into my own dark clods. I am worried about what I will find.

A few weeks before I overheard Josh's conversation with his dad, I had a miscarriage. Together we stood at the front of the sanctuary of our tiny Mennonite Church and shared the news, my body slumping into his. Afterward, in the church basement, gray-haired women patted my arms, whispering their own stories of loss.

Not long after that Josh stopped coming to church altogether. But even with all my doubts and unexamined faith, I kept attending services week after week. The church was there for me when I white-knuckled my way through another pregnancy; women named Edie and Susan and Margaret brought us meals after our son Rowan was born.

In those early years after Josh's deconversion, Sundays were the hardest day of the week. Josh helped when I searched for that mismatched sock or rushed to wipe mouths after breakfast. He made sure the diaper bag was stocked with wipes and slipped a few Kid-Z granola bars in the side pocket.

But when I would leave to walk to church with our two little kids, he loaded his mountain bike into the car instead. We kissed and said goodbye. I walked the kids out the front door and lifted them into the double stroller; I buckled them into their seats and released the brake. On the walk to church it was often windy, and Rowan cried that the sun was in his eyes. I told him to just hold on a little while longer, that we'd be there soon. Eliza sang an off-key version of "Mary Had a Little Lamb," and I thought about that parable of the lost sheep, the one where Jesus leaves the ninety-nine behind in search of the one who has gone astray. I huffed and took deep sighs and put the hat back on the toddler who had just taken it off, and then I put it back on again.

We passed the children's hospital. Two nurses stood on the curb, smoking in matching salmon-colored scrubs. I caught a whiff of second-hand smoke as I kept pushing the heavy stroller that doesn't steer easily, sometimes veering off the sidewalk into brown grass.

Once we arrived at church, I eyed the long flight of stairs up to the sanctuary doors. Like so many buildings in this neighborhood, the church was old, had weathered many winters here, and wasn't designed for twenty-first-century families and all their stuff. I carried my kids one by one up the flight of stairs, readjusting mittens or tightening a boot that threatened to slip off, before pulling the stroller up the concrete steps behind me: thunk, thunk, thunk. We received our bulletin and a soft handshake from a kind-eyed greeter—the same woman who gave us a handmade baby quilt when Eliza was born. I guided my kids into a hard pew and dropped the diaper bag on the crimson cushion.

Eliza sat down, then stood up, then grabbed a hymnal and dropped it, while Rowan decided to lie down on the floor of the sanctuary. I wished I had an extra set of arms, sprouting out of my body like a Hindu goddess, to hold my children close.

Instead I was scrambling and thinking of my husband who was climbing onto a bicycle in a cathedral of trees, his hands gripping handlebars, his body worshipping in wilderness rather than here in this dusty sanctuary. My nose twinged as I held their tiny hands while the pianist played the chords of the first hymn. I hoisted my son onto my hip and rested my cheek against his downy hair.

What am I still doing here? I wondered.

Shortly after Rowan was born, the interim pastor called and asked us about a baby dedication. We'd had Eliza dedicated back when my husband still believed in God. Hand in hand, we'd stood before this very congregation and vowed to raise her in the knowledge of God's vast love for her, that we would tell her the great, old stories of God's work in the history of God's people. Two of our best friends, Meredith and James, now Eliza's godparents, stood beside us just as they had as attendants in our wedding ceremony.

"I just can't do it this time," Josh had told me. "I can't stand in front of the church and pledge our kid to a God I don't believe in."

As I stood for the hymn, I felt the smooth strands of Rowan's hair against my cheek. I felt the heaviness of his body in my arms.

I met my Josh the fall of junior year at Wheaton College. I interviewed him for a school newspaper article because he was coleading a campus-wide week of prayer and fasting to raise awareness and funds for the humanitarian crisis in Darfur. We met in the Stupe, the campus café where students studied and gossiped and held Bible studies. With my borrowed tape recorder rolling, I listened to Josh talk about his simple desire to just *do something* in the face of so much suffering in the world. And what was more powerful than prayer?

I asked my questions and looked into Josh's blue eyes and saw that he was like me, a sincere believer who saw Jesus as the champion of the poor. He was as serious about living his faith as I was. I listened to his desire for change, to his hope for God's justice, and I knew. I knew I wanted to forever bind my life to someone like him, someone who wouldn't settle for an apathetic, ordinary life. We would live in radical contrast to the way most American Christians stumble through their days. And his faith, so blazing and earnest, would bolster and carry mine.

It wasn't long before we were seniors, sitting together on a blanket with our fingers entwined under the flowering magnolia trees on Blanchard lawn. The blossoms were impossibly cheerful; the smell of earth and worms and cut grass was in the air. Classmates strolled past in the way only college students in the springtime can when finals are still weeks away, full of carefree jabber and flirtation, the girls in swishy skirts and sleeveless tops sidling up to the boys in cargo shorts and flip-flops. Two guys tossed a Frisbee back and forth. The sound of guitar music wafted over from another cluster of students lounging on the grass.

We were on our own blanket island, reading the Bible together and pretending to be unaware of people walking by.

"I am the vine; you are the branches," Josh read, pulling his hand away to turn the onionskin page of his Bible. "If you remain in me and I in you, you will bear much fruit; apart from me you can do nothing."

The spiky grass prickled my bare legs as I reached over to re-grasp his hand. He handed me the worn Bible, and I continued reading: "If you do not remain in me, you are like a branch that is thrown away and withers; such branches are picked up, thrown into the fire and burned."

We stared up at those dancing blossoms, inhaled spring's scent, dazed by newfound love and our mutual desire to produce good fruit for God. Later that week we attended the three-hour Easter vigil at the Anglican church we attended, standing on our chairs, ringing bells, and shouting hallelujahs when the priest announced: "He is risen!" Rebirth was all around us; resur-rection reigned. It felt like a guarantee.

All around us we watched our classmates pair off and give one another a "ring by spring." Jokes abounded about young women pursuing their "MRS degree." Many of these campus sayings were caricatures; my girlfriends in college were ambitious and smart and deeply committed to their faith, not boy-crazy husband hunters. But many of us *did* hope we'd meet our mar-riage partners in college or soon thereafter—that we could ring the engagement bell (yes, that's a real tradition at my alma mater) to announce we had found ourselves a Christian spouse. We longed for that mythical godly partner we had learned about in high school youth group, our very own Jim Elliot to our Elisabeth, a Billy Graham to our Ruth.

It's no wonder that, in the jumble of messages I received on Christian marriage, I thought my relationship with God would be amplified by my spouse. When Josh and I fell in love, our shared belief in God was the deepest part of our connection. And I assumed that God would look upon us as a joint spiritual package—that my spiritual fortunes depended in some way on my husband's Christian walk.

If you're not aligned spiritually, then nothing will match up—or so the Christian marriage messaging goes.

When Josh stopped believing in God, I didn't know our mixed-faith marriage was hardly an anomaly. Millions of other married people are doing the hard work of reevaluating their unions after a faith change. A 2015 report from Pew Research showed that more and more marriages are between people of different religious beliefs and that "most generational cohorts actually are becoming less religiously affiliated as they age." The rise of the religious nones suggests that young adults are experiencing faith changes or even abandoning Christianity more now than ever before—which is often a sucker punch for those left in their wake. New conflicts arise as married couples navigate how to spend Sunday mornings, what to teach their children about religion, and how to spend the holidays.

For Christians like me who are married to nonbelievers, finding new models for living a faithful Christian life is often an exercise in frustration. Most churches have married people attending services, yet those who come as singles are often on the sidelines of the community—an experience that unmarried people in the church have long lamented. Add to that the depressing divorce statistics of interfaith marriages (among the highest rates being between evangelicals and religious nones), and the future seems bleak, indeed.

What am I supposed to do now? is the question I asked God the night Josh told his father he wasn't a Christian anymore, and it's the question I've been asking every day since. After so much time in Protestant churches that center on the traditional Christian family, I don't want a self-help guide on how to pray my husband back to faith. Instead, I need hope that my interfaith marriage isn't an affliction I need to bear but a vehicle through which God can move.

God did eventually answer my question, though not in the way I expected. It wasn't by bringing Josh back into the fold (though I still believe in the parable of the lost sheep) but by giving me a place where women don't rely on husbands for their spiritual identities.

God answered my question by giving me a bunch of nuns.

2

BENEDICTINES

*M*y first encounter with nuns came a few years ago, when I started working for the Collegeville Institute, an ecumenical nonprofit located on the grounds of Saint John's Abbey. The abbey is home to one of the largest Benedictine monastic communities in North America. When I was hired, I met with human resources and received a pamphlet on Benedictine values that, beyond having read *The Cloister Walk* by Kathleen Norris, was my first introduction to this ancient form of Christian spirituality. (Norris wrote the bestseller while in residency at the Collegeville Institute. Later I would learn that the abbey had a huge spike in interest from Protestants after Norris's book came out, which they described as "the *Cloister Walk* effect." If you go into the Abbey gift shop today, you can even find a "cloister walk" scented candle made by the monks.) I skimmed the document from HR and, when I got home, stuffed it in a drawer.

It wasn't until one evening, at a special dinner hosted at the abbey, that I reconsidered the relevance of monastic values in my life. Norris was the keynote speaker, and she had agreed to an interview with me for the Collegeville Institute's website the following day.

"I'm going to interview K-Nor herself!!!!" I texted my writing group. They sent celebration emoji and GIFs and even more exclamation points. I felt simultaneously euphoric and nauseous at the prospect of meeting my literary hero, whose books had bolstered me when faith felt tenuous.

I convinced my husband to drive an hour north from our home in Minneapolis to Collegeville for the event, but I immediately regretted it when we stepped inside the banquet hall. My husband was no longer a Christian, and the room was filled with them. Monks, nuns, professors of theology, and other professional religious types were mingling near the refreshment table, sipping from delicate wine glasses and nibbling crackers with cheese. I felt a little awkward seeing my coworkers; I mostly worked from home and was used to interacting with my colleagues through my computer screen. *And who will my husband talk to?* I wondered as I surveyed the crowd.

As the program began, we took our places at assigned seats at a table in the far-right corner. We said our hellos to those we were seated near, inquiring about their connection to the organization honored that night. On the other side of Josh was a woman in her 70s with an enthusiastic grin, slightly oversized teeth, and short, curly, white hair.

"Hello!" she said, shaking our hands and introducing herself as Sister Theresa. I would never have guessed she was a nun from her simple black sweater and gray slacks. We learned she had been on the board of the Collegeville Institute for over a decade and was a member of the women's monastic community at Saint Benedict's Monastery a few miles away.

"For how long?" my husband asked.

"Well, I took my vows when I was eighteen," she replied. "And it will be my sixtieth anniversary soon, my diamond jubilee."

"Wow," we replied, in unison.

The noise in the room made it hard to hear across the table, so I turned to speak with the woman seated to my right—a proud new grandmother who was married to a member of the board. Every so often I would glance over to Josh and Sister Theresa, who were happily chatting away. I heard my husband laugh.

Later, as we were walking out to the parking lot to find our car, I asked Josh, "So how was your conversation with the nun? You two seemed to hit it off."

"She was great," he said. "People are people."

"Did you tell her you weren't a Christian?" I asked him.

"Yeah, I told her that and about my missionary kid background," he replied. "She didn't seem to be concerned. She said that she's a spiritual director and that it's not her place to judge—that everyone is on a journey with God."

"Huh," I said while sliding into the car and clicking on my seatbelt.

Josh drove through campus as the last of the day's sunlight faded around us. It was dark when he turned the car onto the long unpaved driveway, the headlights shining like two bright eyes, that led us to the lakeside apartment where I would be spending the night alone before my interview with Kathleen Norris the following morning.

"Hey," he said as I climbed out of the car and grabbed my overnight bag, "I hope it goes well tomorrow. Don't be nervous, you'll be great. Remember, she's just a person."

I gave him a kiss through the window, resting my cheek against his beard for a beat. "I wish you could stay. I wish you didn't have to work tomorrow."

"Me too," he said, giving me a half hug through the window before turning the car around and starting the long drive back to the city.

The next morning, after a fitful night's sleep, I showed up early to the abbey guesthouse for the interview. I sat on the sleek, modern couches in the lobby, alternatively smoothing my hair and my papers. When I saw Kathleen Norris walking slowly down the hallway, slowed down by a foot injury, I jumped up to offer a jittery hello. She suggested we take our interview upstairs to the guesthouse living room and kitchenette, which she promised never had many visitors this time of day.

As we settled into the room and found a table to prop up Norris's foot, I set up my computer microphone and began asking my carefully prepared questions about her experience as a Benedictine oblate and the challenge of maintaining spiritual practices when a praying community of monks isn't within walking distance. She was gracious and chatty, delving into funny stories about her grandnieces and revealing her love for the Kim Kierkegaardashian Twitter account.

Benedictine spirituality, she told me, is for all of us. Monastic traditions predates major schisms in the church and are, therefore, the common inheritance of all Christians, whether

Orthodox, Catholic, or otherwise. It's a spirituality that she felt no qualms in claiming, even as a Protestant.

As the conversation wound down and we walked back to the front desk of the guesthouse, Kathleen handed me a free copy of *Give Us This Day* from a display stand.

"This," she said, pointing to the monthly Catholic prayer book, "is how I stay connected to the spirituality, even when I can't pray regularly with a monastic community."

As I took the book from her hands and leafed through its pages, I blurted out the question I had been holding.

"But what about your husband?" I asked her, knowing from her books that her late husband was a lapsed Catholic. They had met and married before Norris discerned her call to be a Benedictine oblate, before she reconnected with God and began practicing her faith as an adult. "Was that hard being in different places spiritually?"

"Oh, he made friends with the monks while he was here," she said, waving her hand as if to encompass the whole of the abbey. And that was that.

I thanked her again for the interview and, after she walked away, I stood at the front desk for a while, feeling like I could cry. Why had I thought that this person, esteemed author though she be, would have the answers I was looking for about marriage? And why had I thought it would be appropriate to ask her something so personal?

As I drove home on I-94 past cornfields, pro-life billboards, and the outlet mall, I rehashed the conversation over and over, occasionally hitting the steering wheel with my palm. Norris had seemed unruffled. But why? Maybe she hadn't wanted to talk about such things with a stranger. Yet both she and Sister Theresa showed little concern or fear in engaging with people who had lost faith entirely. Was that a Benedictine thing? It was so unlike the response I saw from the conservative members of our families, who sat Josh down whenever they could and tried to reason with him (making the case for Christ!). It was so unlike my own fear, which wondered if my marriage would crumble without common religious conviction. *If you're not aligned spiritually, then nothing will match up.*

Later at home, I dug out the Benedictine values pamphlet I had unceremoniously buried in my desk drawer a year earlier. Virtues distilled from the Rule of Saint Benedict, such as hospitality, respect for all persons, listening, and stability ("to stand firm in one's promises"), seemed to lend a gentle posture toward religious outsiders while still maintaining a strong, vibrant faith identity.

Whatever those Benedictines had, I wanted it.

So a few months later, I emailed Sister Theresa and asked if I could meet with her for spiritual direction. She invited me to come for an appointment at Saint Benedict's Monastery, which had served as home base for sixty years of her ministry as a professed nun. At the door to her office, Sister Theresa welcomed me, leading me into a room smelling of paper and candle wax, lined with books on theology and liturgy. Several windows framed a small sitting area with two comfortable chairs and a coffee table. After Sister Theresa lit a candle and we sat in silence, I slowly spilled out the story of why I had come.

"We had these Scripture passages read from Isaiah 61 at our wedding," I said. "It was all about this beautiful vision of God redeeming the world. Our whole life together was supposed to be centered on that, about letting God use us to bless others."

Sister Theresa handed me a tissue. I wiped my eyes, then laughed. "God using us," I said. "What does that mean? Was any of that true? Is God even real?"

My laughter left a sharpness to the silence that stretched between us, my doubt hanging in the air.

"Imagine," she said finally, "that God can nourish you. Even in this season. Even through this painful experience."

I closed my eyes and tried to imagine God creating new rivers in a dry desert or changing ashes into beauty like in the Isaiah passage. But I couldn't. When I opened my eyes, my blurry vision instead focused on Sister Theresa who sat a few feet away.

I wondered then if God's nourishment ever came in the form of an elderly nun in a cotton sweater. I wondered if God's redemptive work ever came through sixty years of life shaped by Benedictine monastic rule.

As a parting gift, Sister Theresa gave me a copy of the Rule of Saint Benedict and suggested I journal after reading each section before we met again. This book is not a list of rules to follow but a guide to life, she explained, particularly written by Benedict for his first community of monks to help them live and work together. I held the booklet, so slim that I could slide it in my pocket, with seventy-two very short chapters that cover everything from spiritual practices, what to pray and when, and roles within the monastery. Later I bought a few books on Benedictine spirituality at the Liturgical Press bookstore and made sure to pick up the latest edition of *Give Us This Day*. As I walked back to the car, my new books under my arm, I imagined myself becoming a Benedictine oblate just like Kathleen Norris. I didn't know then how brief my brush with Benedictine spiritual direction would be.

3

October 31

ALL SAINTS' DAY EVE

*I*t was the morning of Halloween when I emailed Sister Theresa to set up another spiritual direction appointment. I had let more than three months pass since I'd cried in her office. Since then, Josh and I had bought our first house in North Minneapolis, and life had gone haywire with packing boxes, our eldest's first day of kindergarten, and transition hiccups that included both a mice infestation and a broken toilet.

In my email, I said I would be driving near Saint Benedict's Monastery later that week for work. Would she have time to meet with me? "O, I am so sorry, Stina," she wrote back, explaining she would be out of town. "Do try again when you are in Collegeville."

I had loved talking with Sister Theresa, but it was becoming obvious that spiritual direction with her wasn't going to be a practice I could regularly sustain. It was hard enough to find time to drive an hour to a Benedictine monastery, let alone coordinate with work and find childcare. And I found that, in the midst of my busy family life, I didn't have the discipline to read the Rule of Saint Benedict on my own. I could barely keep up with the daily *Give Us This Day* readings.

That evening Josh and I were fighting about something or other, but it was Halloween, so we took our bad moods and went trick-or-treating as a family anyway. Eliza, our five-year-old daughter, was dressed as a cat with eyeliner-smudged whiskers; Rowan, our two-year-old son, was dressed as a dinosaur with pointy white teeth framing his face like a bonnet. Josh and I trailed them closely as they knocked on doors and filled plastic buckets with candy in our new city neighborhood, which was often stereotyped as a high-crime area. One neighbor was handing out paper travel cups of apple cider; another passed out Dixie cups of red wine for the grown-ups. Our grumpy moods began to lighten.

I held Rowan's hand as he navigated the steps of a large house down the street in the Old Highland neighborhood, his dinosaur tail wagging with excitement. At the door, a group of fresh-faced college students with shiny ponytails greeted us with jubilant "Happy Halloweens!" They beckoned us onto an enclosed porch, through a narrow hallway, and into a living room.

I followed my son curiously into the strange house, my eyes glued to his swinging tail as he walked straight up to several kind, elderly women holding baskets of candy. One woman, her body slightly bent to one side, asked my children to explain their costumes, which were half-hidden under winter coats and hats. There was something different about this house. As I rubbed my cold hands in the warmth and looked around, it began to click into place: I saw copies of *Give Us This Day* on a side-table, and a framed painting of the biblical characters Elizabeth and Mary embracing on the wall. I was handed a brochure.

"I'm Sister Karen and this is Visitation Monastery," a woman told us in her slightly raspy voice, her warm eyes twinkling, her gray hair curled around her face in a bob. She wasn't wearing a nun's habit, but she did have an oversized silver cross on a chain around her neck.

"Monastery?" my husband asked, turning to me and poking me in the ribs. I shot him a look as I turned back to Sister Karen and explained that we had just bought a house a half mile down the street, that I wasn't Catholic but, as my friend Christiana likes to say, *Catholic-attracted*. I didn't tell her that I was unsuccessfully trying to meet with a Benedictine spiritual director or that I was regularly reading a Catholic prayer book; I didn't tell her that I was struggling to hold on to faith after my husband had lost his faith in God.

"Come for Mass!" Sister Karen implored me, and she pointed to the brochure in my hands. "All the information is on our website."

I said I would as I turned to follow my kids and husband, who were already making their way out the door, down the steps, and back out into the night. The young women on the porch, who I later learned were there for a monastic immersion experience, waved goodbye. As we walked away, I stopped to look back at the house. There was no sign announcing its religious identity, except for a yard sign reading Peace!

"So those were nuns?" my husband asked. Both our childhoods had included multiple viewings of the film *The Sound of Music*, where nuns looked like the Mother Abbess, wearing a black-and-white habit, singing "Climb Every Mountain" to convince Fraülein Maria to return to Vienna. They weren't supposed to invite kids in Halloween costumes into their living rooms. At the very least, I imagined modern sisters to be more like Sister Theresa: living in quiet, contemplative monasteries far away from city neighborhoods like ours.

"Yeah," I replied. "I guess they were."

Later at home, once my kids were asleep, I stole a Snickers bar from the candy basket and looked up the monastery's website. The sisters were not Benedictines but were part of the Visitation Sisters of Holy Mary founded in France four hundred years ago. This particular monastery had sustained a ministry of prayer and presence in the neighborhood for nearly thirty years.

Sister Theresa and Saint Benedict's Monastery were over an hour's drive away, but these nuns were practically next door.

4

SPIRITUAL SINGLENESS

few days after Halloween I got up the gumption to contact the Visitation Sisters. I knew I had to go back. I scrolled through ministry opportunities on their website: retreats, immersion experiences, and something called "Visitation Companions," which was described as a way to "partner with the Sisters in ministry." That sounds right, I thought to myself, then sent a short email asking how I could learn more.

It wasn't until ten days later, when I was at a week-long writing workshop in Massachusetts, that a reply popped into my email inbox after lunch. A woman named Jody wrote to say that my "message was timely" because a new cohort of Visitation Companions was just beginning. She explained that companions must undergo a yearlong spiritual formation process, meeting monthly to pray together and to study the Salesian order to which the sisters belong. Would I be free to stop by the monastery for Mass sometime soon to discuss it?

Yes, I wrote back, explaining that I was out of town but would visit when I returned. Yes, I thought, closing my laptop on the desk in the hotel room. There it was, that feeling. A resonance, a rightness.

I sat on the hotel bed with my copy of *Give Us This Day*, the Catholic prayer book I had been reading on and off ever since Kathleen Norris had handed one to me. I thumbed through, looking for the day's date, crossing the weekly heading: Thirty-Second Week in Ordinary Time. Ordinary Time, I was learning, was a liturgical placeholder for the in-between time. Not Easter or Advent or Lent, just a humdrum Tuesday.

I skimmed the morning prayer, stopping at my favorite daily section called Blessed Among Us. In three short paragraphs, it pays homage to some notable figure in the church—a saint, a martyr, a writer, a nun. In many of these stories, medieval young women with considerable wealth are married and cannot live out their vocation because of their cruel husbands or over-bearing parents. But then the husband dies, or the parents renounce their daughter, and the young woman throws off her familial obligations and joins a monastic order, selling all her possessions and giving her sizable fortune (if she still has one) to found hospitals and schools and charitable works for the poor. In many of these stories, the saintly woman finds new intimacy with God—becoming the bride of Christ, "married" to Jesus.

Some might pity these women with their strange, ascetic practices. Their sexual repression and over-the-top devotions seem, to modern eyes, off-kilter. *Maybe she was just mentally ill,* I thought while reading about Saint Teresa of Ávila, who had mystical unions with the Holy Spirit. Yet I often found myself admiring the gutsy female saints. Most of the women lived in an age when they had little control over their destiny, not having a say in their marriages and no rights to property. Maybe submitting to Jesus and committing to a religious order was a way to reclaim agency in their lives. Less fatalistic weirdos and more like early feminists.

I set down the prayer book and checked the clock by the bed. There was still time for a walk before the next workshop session, so I grabbed my winter coat from the open suitcase on the floor. My hotel was on the grounds of a nature preserve, with marked trails that circled a reservoir. Each day of the weeklong workshop I made myself go outside and walk—away from the stuffy conference room and swivel chairs, away from glowing screens and writerly insecurities.

I stepped out of the dimly lit lobby and into the autumn light. It was a cool November day, one where the light filtered through trees in patches and the wind rustled aspen leaves like pinwheels, and the air felt delicious and brisk as it moved through the woods. Dead brown leaves covered the ground, no longer crisp but old and soggy, like bran flakes left in milk too long, and the walking trail around the reservoir was roped with tree roots, some climbing up, raising their bony knuckles, others slender and snake-like, ready to catch an unassuming ankle or stub an unsuspecting toe.

Before I transferred to Wheaton College as a sophomore, I had attended a small Christian college in Massachusetts, where I spent hours walking in New England woods like these, following skinny mountain-bike trails that led to broad paths that circled ponds. One trail I frequented then led to a ropes course where students lifted their fellow classmates over a tall wooden wall in a group challenge or belayed each other as they walked across elevated logs and rope bridges thirty feet in the air. I had considered everything in those woods as potential metaphors for the spiritual life: the belay rope, the carabiner, the wind in the trees, the climbing wall, the blindfold, the obstacle course, the compass needle always pointing to true north.

This was the language of my faith then, how I grew to understand God and how God worked in the world—through metaphor, through mosquito bites and fighting back tears on the rock wall and awkward team-building exercises. No detail was inconsequential to my meaning-making gaze. A pebble in my shoe was a sin I kept carrying. The half-hidden moon was God's presence, guiding us forward on a hike that had extended long into the night. The twittering of a bird was the praise of creation. And the roots of a tree climbing over rocks or clinging to ledges, or small plants springing up in cracks of boulders, were all signs of God's unrelenting nourishment in stony soil. Likewise, twisting tree branches, the trunks that hunched like a cook over her soup, were always moving to where light fell through canopy. Though the tree sometimes bent over backward, it was wise to reach for sunlight that would become its food.

My faith had been less steady in recent years. I was teetering on the edge of belief and disbelief every day, not always sure which side I would land on.

Yet on this hike I fell into old habits, rambling aloud to God about my uncertain spirituality, about how I didn't know what to believe in. I picked my way around treacherous New England rocks, following the trail until it petered out. The orange blazes marked on trees with spray paint were nowhere to be seen, and the route sputtered into earth and roots. With my eyes always on my feet, always watching for the next step, I had kept myself from tripping, but now I was lost.

"Great," I said aloud. "Just great." Who was I talking to? God? The trees? I checked my phone for the time and wondered whether I would get back before the next workshop started.

A friend of mine once compared adulthood to bushwhacking. There's no highlighted trail on a map telling you where to go and what swampy ground to avoid. Yet Christianity did give us one kind of map, and it's one that Josh and I followed for a long time. Find a Christian spouse. Don't have sex before marriage. Get on the right track by going to church together, joining a small group, and nurturing your mutual spiritual growth through Bible study. Do all these things, follow these rules, take these surefire paths, and you will protect yourself from sin and danger and brokenness.

But, for me, adulthood and grown-up faith has meant bush-whacking. I wonder if it's that's way for everyone, even for those who mostly follow the straight and narrow and do the "right" things. Some kind of disappointment will upend your life sooner or later, whether it be divorce or infertility or illness or adultery or unemployment or plain old selfishness. Franciscan Richard Rohr writes that the first half of life is when your childhood understanding of faith and default mode of operating work just fine. For many, it's in the second half of life that it all falls apart and something has to give. There needs to be a new way of operating, of being in the world, that embraces the messiness of a life no one expected to be living.

There is no trail here, but I kept walking, kept my eyes on my feet and the twisted, gnarled roots. As I made my own path along the water, I thought about the nuns on Fremont Avenue, about the sisters at Saint Benedict's Monastery, about wild women saints that served God in miraculous ways. I wondered why I was so attracted to them and their work.

The light shifted, and fragments of sunshine sliced through the air around me like shards of glass. I stopped, my senses heightened: the sound of water along the shore, the smell of cold wind, the feel of tree roots under my sneakers. I listened to my own breath. It was a singular moment, almost holy. Were the nuns praying right now? The light continued to shift, illuminating new circles of earth around my feet.

Then something remarkable happened. I heard the words "spiritual singleness," right there in the middle of the woods. Two words I had never put together before were now in my consciousness, ex nihilo. I sensed a puzzle piece clicking into place.

Where had the words come from? Were they from God? Was it just my subconscious making connections under the waters, sending up a missive?

Maybe that's what this is about. The celibate nuns, the saints, my clinging to faith, my desire to partner with the sisters in my neighborhood. Somehow the nuns had figured out a way to God without an earthly husband. *I'm spiritually single, and so are they.*

I stopped to type the phrase into my phone, sending myself a text message so I wouldn't forget. I stuck my phone into my back pocket, then turned to face the woods. An orange blaze was just now visible through the trees.

5

November 29

DOROTHY DAY

I didn't tell Josh about the spiritual singleness episode in the woods. I wasn't sure how to explain it to him; I wasn't even sure how to understand it myself. All I knew was that I needed to return to Visitation Monastery.

"Come for Mass," Sister Karen had said on Halloween, and I finally took her up on her invitation in late November. That, and Jody had emailed me again about the spiritual formation group for those interested in becoming Visitation Companions. An informational meeting would be held after the service.

When I stepped outside my back door, my heavy winter coat stayed in the closet. The weather was unseasonably mild in Minnesota; the forecast said it would hit sixty degrees. Our neighbor had a new wreath hanging on the front door, and our own Christmas tree was already up in the alcove, heavily decorated with ornaments on the bottom third, where our kids could reach the branches.

I was too late to walk, and I couldn't quite remember what the monastery looked like, so I typed the address into Google maps and drove down Fremont half a mile, slowing down when my phone said, "Your destination is on the right."

There it was. The yellow house with its Peace sign in the yard, a house that didn't look all that different from its neighbors. Easily missed, like Harry Potter's platform nine and three-quarters. I climbed the two flights of stairs up to the monastery's front door. A discreet sign was in the window, reading The Sisters Are at Prayer. Shoot. Even with the four-minute drive, I still managed to be late for the 8 a.m. service.

I pushed open the door and made my way onto a front porch with a neatly stacked pile of firewood to one side and a set of white wicker patio furniture on the other. Everything looked bright in the morning light. The next door, leading into the monastery, was locked. It was a solid door with dark brown wood, probably original to the house, which was likely built over a hundred years ago like the others in this neighborhood. I rapped my knuckles on the glass.

A tall woman wearing khaki slacks and a button-down blouse appeared through the window and opened the door, letting me inside a long hallway.

"We've already started," she said in a hushed voice.

"I'm sorry to be late," I said.

The woman smiled and beckoned me down the hallway to an opening. I followed her, wondering if she was one of the nuns. Stairs to the right. A dozen visible people seated in chairs to the left, their backs to me. She handed me a blue hymnal and offered me an open chair. When she dragged a heavy chair over and placed it beside my own, I realized that she must have given me her seat.

Someone was talking, but I couldn't see far into the room from where I sat. The house had been built long before open-concept floor plans were in vogue. I could see just part of the living room where the nuns had handed out candy on Halloween and, when I strained my neck, I caught a glimpse of an altar set up with a white cloth. Around twenty people sat in a large circle around the edge of the room, some in easy chairs and couches. They were listening, so I listened too.

I can't remember many of the details of that first Mass at Visitation Monastery. I don't remember who sat next to me, or what I talked about with others after the service. I can't recall the songs we sang or what I did with my hands when everyone else crossed themselves on their foreheads, lips, and hearts before the Gospel reading.

But I do remember a few things: a time of prayer for a homeless couple that had come to the monastery's door earlier in the week. A hymn that Sister Karen led on her guitar. After a priest gave the homily, one woman reflected on the strangely warm, in-between season we were in. (Later I would learn that it's not typical for people to share openly during Mass and other daily prayer services, but this was a practice of Visitation Monastery.) She admonished the group not to rush into Advent. Instead, enjoy this Thirty-Fourth Week in Ordinary Time. Extend the Thanksgiving holiday another week.

After Mass I stood around with a paper cup of coffee, waiting for the Visitation Companions meeting. Jody, the lay leader of the companions, and Sister Suzanne walked me downstairs into the basement. There must have been some of the others from the formation group, Jane or Kristin or Kathie, but the details are fuzzy in my memory. We must have talked about the one-year spiritual formation process ahead of us: about meeting monthly to learn about Salesian spirituality, about the history of the order and of its founders, Saint Jane de Chantal and Saint Francis de Sales.

All I remember with any clarity is Sister Suzanne, sitting in a blue chair, telling a story about brushing her teeth next to Dorothy Day during some activist trip she took in the 1970s. Dorothy Day was the one Catholic I knew something about, having read her memoir *The Long Loneliness* and volunteered alongside Josh in a ministry that was inspired by the Catholic Worker communities that Day helped found in the 1930s.

I took one picture that morning. It was of a book on the coffee table called *Saved by Beauty*, about Dorothy Day's spiritual journey. I sent the photo to the women in my writers' group with the text: *Went to Mass. Dorothy Day is all over this place, so you know these nuns are very cool.*

I didn't know that the book was on the coffee table because it was Dorothy Day's death day. She is not canonized as a saint by the Catholic Church (though many have taken up that cause), but she was another *single* woman who lived out her faith in radical, unconventional ways.

It felt like another sign that I was in the right place.

6

NEW MONASTICISM

*W*hen I tell my friend Meredith that I've started hanging around a monastery, she says she's not surprised.

"Stina," she says, "you've always been into that new monasticism stuff. Remember Shane Claiborne?"

Ah yes. Shane Claiborne. When Josh and I were in college, Shane came and spoke at one of our chapel services. He was a white guy with dreadlocks and patched jeans; he told stories about living in solidarity with homeless people and embracing a life of downward mobility. When he spoke about the intentional Christian community that he and a bunch of college friends had formed in Philadelphia, my peers in the chapel seats took notes. Shane told tales of hosting neighborhood barbecues, running afterschool programs, and doing circus tricks during community block parties. His stories sounded a lot like the parables that Jesus told, and his community sounded a lot like heaven.

I wasn't the only one at my college enamored with Shane's vision of intentional community. When I was a junior, I was close with a group of seniors who shared common values—community, social justice, simplicity—and wanted to live them out together. The group met a few times over the spring semester, ultimately deciding to look for a big house to rent in Chicago after graduation. When I returned to college for my senior year, those friends had found jobs in the city and moved in together. Some of the students already had connections in North Lawndale, where a Christian community health clinic and church worked in partnership to promote wellness in a high-poverty community.

So a new intentional community house was born—they named it the Kedzie House for the street where they found a rental. It was the heyday of the new monasticism movement in the mid-2000s Protestant church, and young-adult cohousing communities were springing up like dandelions.

The new monasticism movement inspired a generation of mostly white Protestants, like me, who were looking for another way to be a Christian. We didn't want to follow the expected trajectory: buy a single-family house in the suburbs, take the occasional vacation to Florida, coach little league. It didn't help that many of us graduated from college into the recession of the mid-2000s, where high paying jobs were rare and the ethics of unpaid internships were unquestioned. Living cheap in those early post-college years was a necessity.

I recently reread *School(s) for Conversion: 12 Marks of a New Monasticism*, an anthology of essays about the distinctive attributes of the movement published in 2005. Chapters by new monasticism leaders like Shane Claiborne and Jonathan Wilson-Hartgrove inspired me all over again with their stories of radical welcome. But when I went to look at the website referred to in the book, I found that the domain newmonasticism.org was for sale. I wondered then how many of the young adults inspired by new monasticism ten years ago had flamed out like me.

If you asked me why Josh and I were inspired by new monasticism, I would tell you about Shane Claiborne, sure, but I would also tell you about the faith we shared then—about how Josh once told me that shoveling snow was the best part of his prayer life. He was reading books about the holiness of work and prayer. He embraced a fully embodied faith. It is a very monastic concept—to toil in the monastery's gardens, to bake bread or brew beer for the monastery's business, to cut trees and craft furniture or keep bees or distill sugar maple sap into syrup as an act of prayer. We both felt a calling to live our Christian faith in community; we both romanticized life and work outside the mainstream in the alternative economy.

When Josh was a Christian, he would write Psalms on notecards and have them delivered to me on our college campus. He loved to make pottery, to fix and ride bikes, and sit on the back of a tractor at the organic farm where he worked for three growing seasons after we got married. And at night he would read volumes by Teilhard de Chardin or Henri Nouwen or Jacques Ellul. When we spent six months apart in college (me volunteering in a refugee camp in Kenya and Josh serving with a mission team in an urban slum in Venezuela), we wrote prayers of blessing to each other nearly every day.

After graduating from college, we didn't join the Kedzie House community in Chicago, but we did belong to a house church with other young wannabe radicals in Minneapolis. We didn't make much on our AmeriCorps stipends and nonprofit salaries, but our Sunday night dinners and Tuesday night prayers made us feel rich. We hosted clothing swaps and craft nights and went on long bike rides around the chain of urban lakes. I never felt lonely; there was always a weekly potluck to go to. Soon after our wedding, the house church fizzled, and our faith began its slow drift. We started dreaming of something bigger, of buying a farm, maybe (we were all reading Wendell Berry, of course), or driving out to Philadelphia to join Shane Claiborne's community.

So less than a year into our marriage, Josh and I left Minneapolis and spent five months at Jubilee Partners. Jubilee is an intentional community in rural Georgia, where it sits on 280 acres of a former cotton plantation. Its red soil was depleted from decades of cotton farming, but the mostly Mennonite community members have fed organic material back into a two-acre garden plot, building up the nutrients into loamy, brown dirt that supports a plentiful sweet potato harvest. The acre plot of blueberry plants is tended carefully; shovelfuls of pine needles have been heaped around the base of each plant, adding back the necessary acidity for them to bear fruit.

I was attracted to Jubilee's ministry to recently arrived refugees and Josh to organic farming. For five months, we pitched hay in grassy fields together. We wore bandanas on our heads and cooked gigantic vegetarian meals in the community kitchen: pizza with homemade dough, baked potatoes with à la carte toppings, groundnut stew with pumpkin and peanut butter. I learned how to make twelve loaves of bread at a time using the *Simply in Season* cookbook. We taught basic English to people from Burma and Mexico and the Congo using laminated flashcards and bingo games. We sang "Old McDonald" and nursery songs to the children, read *Green Eggs and Ham*, and practiced basic conversations: "Hello! How are you?" "I'm fine, thank you."

Those of us who were volunteers lived in awe of the older, wiser Christian radicals, some of whom had founded the community thirty years prior and had found a way to live in an interdependent, communal way for the long haul. Josh and I particularly admired one Mennonite couple who were just a few years older than we were. He was a classic farmer who wore suspenders and took care of the cows and goats, and she had long, brown hair down to her elbows and tended the plant nursery.

One late winter morning, the cohort of volunteers gathered in the library for a meeting. Some sat on the floor, others on the couches, others on mats that rested directly on the ground. A fire crackled in the fireplace, and I cupped a mug of weak coffee from the community kitchen, settling into my spot on the floor. Over the course of our volunteer term, partners shared their life story with our volunteer group, and today it was the young farmer's turn. He was generally so quiet, I was curious about what he might say.

"When I first came to Jubilee Partners it was like Christmas every day," he said. "I thought, What is this place? How can I stay here forever?"

He shook his head. "I never knew how painful a place like this could be."

I leaned forward in my chair and looked over to catch Josh's eye from across the room, but he wasn't looking at me. We had been talking about staying at Jubilee ourselves, committing to live as novices for a year. During that process, we would discern whether we were called to become long-term members of the community. Though we, too, thought life at Jubilee was like Christmas morning, I couldn't help noticing how tired all of the partners seemed and how reticent some were to get to know us, the ever-rotating community of volunteers. Some underlying tension, some undercurrent of pain, rippled through our conversations. We heard that a key family had recently left, leaving behind torn relationships and lingering resentment.

The young farmer spoke about the trials of community living, the frustrations, the endless meetings to decide if movies were permitted in the community or if both cake and ice cream could be served at birthdays (normally ice cream was restricted to just two evenings a month). Managing the land was a joy but also hard when other community members didn't understand the investments that needed to be made. The Georgia climate was hot, and fire ants swarmed the soil.

Clarence Jordan, founder of the Koinonia community in nearby Americus, Georgia, wrote about intentional community as an alternative model of living, meant to be a "demonstration plot for the Kingdom of God." Maybe not everyone would join one, but the communities pointed to the prophetic nature of Christianity. They showed that another way was possible.

But we were learning that even in our ideal community that practiced radical hospitality, there was suffering and pain. For all their hardships, the young farmer and his wife stayed at Jubilee Partners, choosing to continue their ministry in the community instead of walking away. But the cost—the struggle—scared us and so, when our five-month volunteer term at Jubilee was over, we went home to Minneapolis. Still, in those early years of our marriage, we talked often of going back.

I only visited the Kedzie House a handful of times, but what I remember is this: trash along the boulevard and in the gutter, neighborhood kids running in and out the front door, my friend Shea washing dishes at the kitchen sink. I stood beside her as she rinsed dinner plates, listening to her talk about her job in the community health clinic, about her plans to apply for medical school. The others in the house held a hodgepodge of jobs: AmeriCorps volunteer, ESL teacher, barista, nonprofit grunt. They had meals together a few times a week.

The community lasted for a few years until people started getting married or getting into graduate school or getting tired of community meetings and sharing bathrooms with seven other people. I'm not sure if the residents of the Kedzie House prayed together regularly, but they did embody many of the "twelve marks of a new monasticism," which outlined principles such as "hospitality to the stranger" and "relocation to abandoned corners of the empire." To join a new monastic community, you didn't need to be celibate or a member of the

Catholic Church, nor did you have to take a vow of obedience to an authoritative abbot or abbess. Each community had its own process for accepting new members, but they were not as regulated as the ones that Catholic sisters undergo before joining a religious community. They were not lifelong vows.

For young Catholic women who feel the call to simplicity and service, who want to live in a big old community house after college, there's a different model. They can go on a discernment tour and visit the Carmelites, the Dominicans, and the Franciscans, comparing rules of life, exploring monastic versus apostolic communities. There are vocation directors to guide them and novitiate years to undergo. Instead of creating something new, these young idealists submit to hierarchies and read spiritual masterpieces like the Rule of Saint Benedict on life in community.

Plenty of women start the process to become nuns and then decide to leave, but some stay and make vows and live their whole lives in the rhythm of prayer and service. The institution's stability is what makes the call to community last, because there is support enough to see it through. There is wisdom baked into the structure itself. I wonder now if God calls some to be monks in every generation. New monasticism and other experiments in community are what happen when your tradition doesn't have an established outlet for that vocation.

But vowed religious life is often viewed as useless by those on the outside, especially the life of cloistered communities that make prayer their primary activity. Why waste your life praying all the time? Why forgo sex and money and autonomy? What is the meaning of a life spent cloistered behind a grille, ensconced in a nun's habit, teaching elite Catholic girls their grammar lessons?

It seems to me that the new monastics focused more on social justice than on developing a contemplative lifestyle centered on spiritual disciplines. They hosted homework clubs for neighborhood kids, tended community gardens, and provided temporary housing for the homeless. Communities like the Kedzie House had more in common with the settlement house movement of the late 1800s and early 1900s, popularized by Jane Addams's Hull House (where modern social work was born), than with cloistered communities that rose at four to sing morning prayers. New monasticism was good with its theology of social action, on solidarity with the poor, on hospitality to the stranger, but sometimes lost when it came to the contemplative center of these traditions.

Intentional communities often fail. Some of the new monastic communities latched onto ancient traditions, like the Rule of Saint Benedict, in an attempt to create a more sustainable structure to guide community life and even developed a popular book of common prayer for "ordinary radicals." Most of the communities featured in the book *12 Marks of New Monasticism*, like the Simple Way, Reba Fellowship, and the Rutba House, are still going strong.

I wonder now if the Kedzie House failed for the same reasons that Josh and I didn't go back to Jubilee Partners after our volunteer term. Living in community is hard work, and without vows to keep us there, who would want to stick it out?

In the evangelical worship services of my youth, I sang with other Christians, asking God to "set my heart on fire." We were "sold out" for Jesus. Our churches encouraged us to throw ourselves into whatever passions God had given us in order to love and serve God better. For many years I was nothing if not earnest about my faith, about following Jesus with every ounce of my life.

This spirit of passion was characteristic of my peers in the new monastic movement as well. We were inspired; we were idealistic. We wanted to actually live the way Jesus did; we wanted to be like the early church and share everything among ourselves. But old-school monastics knew something that most of us didn't: passion can only get you so far when you encounter inevitable struggle and pain. Most hot and holy fires are unsustainable.

In the months after I visited Sister Theresa for spiritual direction, I finally sat down and read the Rule of Saint Benedict. Instead of "following your passion," the Rule values stability. It teaches that "all things are to be done with moderation." Accepting your limits—that one cannot sustain a high level of engagement or enthusiasm 100 percent of the time—is the only means to living a consistent, centered life for God.

I wonder now what a modern worship song about the Benedictine values of moderation and stability would sound like. Instead of "I will go, Lord, where you lead me," we would sing, "I will stay put, Lord, and remain faithful in my daily tasks."

Instead of "Open the eyes of my heart, Lord," we would sing, "Help me to rest and say no, Lord."

Those revised lyrics are not sexy, not at all like the church retreats, the summer camps, the special seminars that throughout my teens and early twenties ignited my idealism into a giant flame. I would return home each summer from camp certain that *this* would be the time my life would be transformed. I would set high goals for myself and then crash with disappointment at the inevitable letdown.

When Josh left Christianity, much of our shared idealism went with it. We stopped having "maybe, someday" conversations of returning to Jubilee Partners; we no longer wrote prayers of blessing for one another. I grew cloudy with disillusionment, no longer able to see a way to live out my faith in the countercultural or communal way I'd hoped I would.

But when I discovered that the Visitation Sisters were in the neighborhood, it was as if God was winking at me. My dreams of joining a new monastic community may have been gone, but *look!* God seemed to be saying. Here are some actual, old-school monastics for you to befriend—the real deal. Go learn something solid from their rhythm of life with God, something that has stood the test of time. Maybe the stability of their vow had something to teach me about marriage.

7

WAITING IN THE DARK

*J*osh and I never joined an intentional community for the long haul, but we did start a nuclear family: two little kids, a mortgage, a cat. We comanaged our finances; we did the grocery shopping, cooking, school drop-offs, and cleaning. We held house meetings and made chore charts and took turns picking nostalgic favorites for movie nights.

A marriage, a family, is an intentional community too, of course, but unlike Jubilee Partners or a monastery, our family didn't have a rule of life, especially after Josh deconverted. We were making it up as we went along. The Kielsmeier-Cook family culture was a mishmash of agnosticism and Christianity and middle-class American values. We were mostly winging it.

I wish I could say that Josh and I have the interfaith family rituals thing down, but we don't. We've tried. Well, I've tried—I am not always sure whether he's really interested, or just going along because it's important to me.

Shortly after I met the nuns, as December came around, I began to scroll past photos of candles being lit by cheerful children and family devotionals for sale on social media. In a last-minute panic, I picked up a cheap package of four green votive candles from Aldi. I downloaded "A Simple Advent Guide" for kids from the internet and informed my family that we would start our own nightly Scripture readings and light candles before diner. Like I said, we were winging it.

"Okay, everyone," I said, the PDF of the Advent guide pulled up on my computer, the laptop resting on my knees. The table was set, a plate piled with chicken quesadillas at the center next to a lonely bowl of cherry tomatoes. Four green candles were there, wicks white and waxy. Eliza was in the living room, looking at a picture book about dragons who eat tacos; beside her Rowan was carefully drawing in his PJ Masks coloring book. Josh was in the bathroom.

"Everyone," I said again, calling to them, trying to draw them to me, like a beacon to a fleet of wayward ships. "Come to the table. It's time for our Advent readings."

Eliza poked her head up, like a turtle from its shell, and said, "What?"

I repeated myself now for the third time. Josh walked into the room.

"Ready?" I said to him.

"Sure," he said, then gently prodded our son to put away his coloring book. Rowan squawked and gripped the crayons in his fists.

"Mom," Eliza said, walking over to the table and picking up a candle. "What are these for? Can I light one?"

I assured her she could once everyone was ready and once they were seated. I took the electric lighter, the kind with a long stem, and showed my daughter how to set the wick on fire. She delighted at this new power, at watching something catch flame.

With everyone ready, I launched into a short explanation of Advent: how we light candles and wait during the month of December to prepare ourselves for the One who will be born. I scrolled through "A Simple Advent Guide" and read the opening Psalm, this one from Psalm 146. The psalm is about the triumph of the godly and those who place their hope in God.

The next step in our Advent celebration was a question we were all supposed to answer: Where did I see God today?

Eliza asked, "What does that mean? I never see God, or Jesus," and I tried to explain that "seeing" God is about looking for moments in our day when we feel most alive, most at peace. That God made us to live abundantly, so when life is abundant God is there.

Rowan was about to turn three and didn't quite understand the assignment, so he said: "I see God in church!" even though it was a Thursday. As we went around the table, Eliza talked about seeing God when a friend shared her snack at school. Josh said that he saw God in the wind today, the way it whipped through the barren tree branches and sent leaves scattering. I smiled.

"How about you?" Josh asked me. "I see God here," I said, looking him in the eyes. His smile matched mine, a mirror across the dining room table, and we held our gaze until Rowan picked up a quesadilla and started to tear off pieces of the flour tortilla and throw them in the air, and Eliza reached over to the lit candle and dragged it close to her plate.

"Wait! We're not done!" I said, pushing the candle away and taking the quesadilla from Rowan's hand.

The next step in "A Simple Advent Guide" was to listen to a song. I clicked on the link and "Praise to the Lord" by Sara Groves opened in Spotify. I turned up the volume on the laptop at the opening bars of piano and strumming guitar. Sara Groves's sweet voice sang out the words to the old hymn and we listened together:

> All that has life and breath, come now with praises
> > before Him
> Let the Amen sound from His people again
> Gladly forever adore Him.

The song was only three minutes long, but it dragged on. The kids wiggled but I could tell they were listening, and Josh was too.

I only rarely played Christian music in the house, and when I did it was of the folk acoustic variety. Playing Advent music was laying claim to the airspace in our agnostic-Christian home, but in that particular moment it felt okay. Was it okay because Josh saw God in the wind today? Maybe. I knew he was uncomfortable on some level, but tonight he was playing along. He was listening to the hymn and sharing from his heart and for once, I was grateful I dragged us all into Advent.

This nightly rhythm continued most nights of the week leading up to Christmas. Just before supper we gathered around our antique wooden table, the one with tiny crumbs lodged into the crack along the center. We sat and the kids took turns lighting candles, and I read Scriptures. We listened to music—to hymns, Zechariah's song, songs about how all will be well, about how God remembers his eternal covenant despite all the evidence to the contrary. About God's mercy shining brighter than the sun.

And as I looked around me at my family's shining faces, at the flicker of candlelight, as I heard the guitar and words of peace, of joy, of hope drifting from the tiny computer speakers, I sensed God with us.

Many of my friends have gone through deconstruction of their faith—some have stopped going to church entirely, others only on occasion. And I get it, I really do. Why keep showing up when sleeping in on Sundays is so much more enjoyable? Why cajole the kids out of their pajamas, rush through the breakfast dishes, and venture out into the snow and slush, instead of letting the children play with Legos and letting yourself read a magazine or call your sister or bake zucchini bread?

Maybe it's my stubborn streak, or maybe it's the Holy Spirit, I can't really tell, but I think knowing that this is my mantle, my responsibility to either raise these kids with religion or not—it has made me march those kids into the car, to scrape the windshield, to brave the snowy highways most Sundays. It's a reflex. After all, if I don't take my kids to church, they don't go. If I don't read the *Jesus Storybook Bible* to them, they won't learn about Jesus feeding the five thousand or King David's Psalms or about how Lazarus got up and walked.

Despite my doubts about God, despite the ways I have watched my certainties unravel like a slowly pulling thread, I still attend Sunday services most weeks. I wonder sometimes whether, if Josh had been less resolute about denying faith, I would have just drifted away from religious practices like the rest of them. Some days I wonder whether, without the holy fear of my kids growing up not knowing God's great love for them, not knowing any kind of tradition or community, I would have gradually stopped participating in a faith community.

"Where did you see God today?" the Advent guide had us ask, and it's a question I've been asking myself too. If God is love, then seeing God is a lot like seeing love. And love assumes the best in others—it looks at my agnostic, disbelieving husband with the clear-eyed, unconditional belief that he is doing the best he can. That he is at the particular part of his journey where he needs to be; that, as Sister Theresa said a few months ago at Saint John's Abbey, God is walking with us regardless of what particulars we believe at any given moment, and life is long. Who knows where, exactly, we will end up?

But then one night we read from Psalm 32, and I choked out the last few verses of the Scripture reading: "Therefore, let all the godly pray to you while there is still time, that they may not drown in the floodwaters of judgment." I said the words, shifted in my seat, thankful my kids were too young to ask me who, exactly, will drown in the floodwaters. Josh didn't say anything after the verses were read, just folded his arms, and I rushed on to the next part.

"Where did you see God today?" I asked. Rowan repeated his usual response: "I saw God in church!" and Eliza said that today she wasn't sure.

"I'm not sure God was there today," she said. "I mean, I can't see him. I don't know where the love was strong."

I told her that's okay. I told her that sometimes I don't feel God's love either.

"Just because you don't feel it," I said, "doesn't mean it's not there."

I felt Josh's eyes on me, but he didn't say anything. When it was his turn, he said he didn't feel like participating tonight.

I pushed onward, ready to wrap up this family ritual, ready to return to safer waters. "Okay, well, I feel God's love here now, in this room," I said, repeating myself, but I was lying. I felt like a fraud. Then I turned on the music, and the chords were in the same key as every cheesy worship song from the Christian radio station I heard growing up, and I wanted to just slam down the computer lid right then and there, cutting off the music, aborting this moment that just wouldn't happen the way I wanted it to. Still, I was grimly determined to keep going, so we listened to the first verse until even I couldn't stand it anymore, then I clicked the Stop button and carried the computer back to my desk.

After dinner we put the kids to bed, and I stayed up late cleaning the kitchen while Josh read in the other room. I listened to a podcast so I didn't have to face my thoughts. When it was late I walked past the table on my way to bed and remembered the failure of that evening.

This year, Advent feels like pain, like absence, like wanting to know God's great love and coming up empty. It feels a lot like waiting in the dark.

8

December 24

CHRISTMAS EVE

*I*t was the first Christmas Eve since I'd met the nuns, and our plans kept changing. At first we were going sledding before the candlelight service, then we decided to meet up with friends, then those friends invited us to another gathering just a few blocks from Calvary, the American Baptist Church where I had only recently started going on Sundays. After seven years as a member of the small, tight-knit Mennonite congregation, I'd made the painful decision to switch churches six months earlier. That's how I found myself on this holiest of nights pulling into the driveway of a strange house to spend the holiday with people I barely knew. And they were church people.

The car door slammed open and I unbuckled Eliza from her car seat, slipping the harness from her winter coat. Josh carried Rowan on his hip as we navigated icy steps. Our hosts were kind, meeting us at the door and showing us where we could stash our boots and mittens. Inside, people lingered around a large kitchen island covered in dishes: a platter of cheese and crackers, a ceramic bowl of vegetarian Swedish meatballs, and plates of homemade Christmas cookies. I had sent Josh to Aldi before it closed early to pick up something to bring, and in he carried a cheap salami and cheese platter. It wasn't homemade, this wasn't home, and it was freaking Christmas Eve.

I sipped a glass of red wine and made small talk, my eyes darting to my children as they joined the chaotic play of the others, gleefully dumping out boxes of toys on the floor. Rowan, who had just turned three, was potty-training. Every ten minutes or so I walked by and whispered into his ear, "Do you need to go?" "NO!" he said, throwing a hand in the air. "Okay!" I said, backing away before confirming that his pants were, indeed, dry.

My cheeks flushed, I chatted and introduced myself to people I didn't know and thanked the hosts again for including us relative strangers at the last minute. Josh seemed to be holding his own with this group of Christians, talking about Marvel movies and the travails of bike commuting in the winter. I was new to this congregation and wanted these church people to like us, to see us as normal, even though only I attend services while Josh stays home.

Soon someone announced that it was time for the candlelight service at church a few blocks away, so we scrambled to put on our hats and coats. Eliza cried that she couldn't find her mittens, but after a few minutes of futile searching I said, "I'm sure they will turn up later." Outside the cold air stung my eyes and I held tightly to Josh's arm and, while passing our parked car, we discovered our daughter's missing mittens lying in the snow. I smiled at him, and he said, "It's a Christmas miracle!" Lost, then found. Our kids shrieked and ran down the salted sidewalks with our friends' children, and we took turns guiding them away from the busy street, herding them toward the church.

The sanctuary smelled of pine trees and glowed with lights, the pews filled with husbands like mine, who only attend church services on Christmas or Easter. The pastor was in a suit and women wore Nordic sweaters and men had on button-downs with khakis. I only recognized a few faces in the crowd.

We took the stairs to the balcony, finding our way in the dark, shushing our children as they talked loudly to each other in excitement. My good friends Bonnie and Luke were in-between churches and decided to attend the candlelight service here, too. Their kids and ours grabbed hands and started crawling over pews. Another child discovered crayons and paper in the back and soon a clot of kids was lying on their stomachs, drawing.

"Just let them be," Josh whispered as I tried to steer my daughter back to the pew. I sunk into the hardbacked seat, trying to concentrate on the sermon, wondering what my friends Bonnie and Luke thought of the church, wondering what Josh was feeling, wondering if this plan had been worth it.

"That's mine!" said a child's voice from the back, ringing loud as a bell. I got up again to tell the kids, in my most ferocious whisper, "For the last time, be quiet."

That's when I saw my son, a strained looked on his face. I grabbed his torso, then pulled back the elastic on his pants. Oh no. Why had I thought tonight was a good night for underwear?

"Let me get you out of these," I said to him, leading him to a private back corner of the balcony with the diaper bag over my shoulder. As I changed his clothes, I laughed under my breath. At least it's fitting, I thought. Baby Jesus probably peed his pants on Christmas too.

When the closing hymn mercifully came, we walked down to the main floor and an usher handed out candles with those paper turtlenecks to keep the wax from dripping onto your fingers. We sang "Silent Night" as our children gleefully waved lit candles. *Who thought this was a good idea?* I wondered, crouching down to push back their hands when the candles got too close to their faces. My heart pounded, and I started to sweat under my heavy sweater. I shot a look at Josh. He apparently had decided not to fight this parenting battle with me but was standing upright and, of all things, singing the words to the hymn. Just great. Of all the people in this family who get to sing "Silent Night" on Christmas Eve, surely the Christian should be the one?

We clomped back out into the dark night, back a few blocks to our car. When the door slammed shut, I exhaled, long and slow.

"That was kind of a disaster," I said.

Josh kept his eyes on the road but reached out to grab my mittened hand and gave it a squeeze. I looked back at the kids in the backseat and I wondered what memories they'd have of church, of Christmas—of their family in these awkward situations, never quite fitting anywhere. I turned to look out the window and watched the gray snowbanks blur as we drove through streetlamp pools of light.

9

MOSCOW SPIRITUALITY

One afternoon in January, while packing up the last of the Christmas stockings and twinkle lights, I listened to a radio segment about how Moscow only had six minutes of sunlight for the entire month of December, the least amount of light for that city in recorded history. The announcer asked if those six minutes were all at once and the reporter responded: "Oh, it was painfully meted out over a number of days. You could enjoy just every thirty seconds or so as it came by."

I shook my head. Only six minutes of sunlight for an entire month? I may live in the freezing Midwest, but at least we get blue skies with our negative thirty degrees wind-chill.

But the idea of catching a glimpse of light in several-second intervals—that resonates on a different level. The last few years have felt like one long, gray December after decades of summer; the unknowing, the disillusionment, the fallout after Josh's loss of faith has obscured any certainty that God is there, or cares. Yet I can't deny that there have also been moments when rays break through, the occasional burst of light to remind me that, indeed, the sun is still there. That I can trust in a God who loves us both deeply no matter what Josh believes.

The older I get, the more Moscow seems like a metaphor for the spiritual life. Mother Teresa famously experienced crippling spiritual drought for years of her ministry; most religious people, if they're honest, will confess to times of great distance from God's presence. For whatever reason, faith can become more distant as we travel through life, encountering disappointment and twisty turns. We live in a Moscow world, and we're all looking for the light.

Like many of my generation, I haven't felt particularly rooted in one Christian tradition. I was baptized Presbyterian and was raised mainline Protestant, yet I was "saved" at a Billy Graham crusade and went to Bible camp every summer. I spent four years at evangelical colleges and attended a charismatic Anglican church, where I learned about both liturgy and how to raise my hands during a worship song. After graduation, Josh and I bounced from an Episcopal church to Jubilee Partners, finally landing in a small, service-oriented Mennonite congregation where I stayed for seven years. The congregation rented space in a historic Lutheran building near the children's hospital, and we loved that we could walk to church each Sunday. It was the last church Josh and I attended together as Christians.

When its lease expired and the little Mennonite church started looking for a new building to rent outside Minneapolis, I started looking for a church to attend in the city. Josh wasn't a Christian at this point, and it was my first time going "church shopping" alone. I checked out the one with an emphasis on racial reconciliation, the emergent one with a circular couch floor plan and art on every wall, the reverent Episcopal one that allowed me to slip in and out unnoticed. All of these churches were fine, but I quietly balked at all the new faces, the unfamiliar songs and nursery workers, the loneliness of visiting a place without my husband at my side. It seemed like too much work to start over, to introduce myself to strangers as Stina, who goes to church with her two children while her husband stays at home.

Around the time Josh and I first met Sister Theresa at Saint John's Abbey, I started regularly attending Calvary. When it came to church, I was only looking for a few things: some people I already knew, a great youth education program, racial and economic diversity, and a commitment to Minneapolis. Calvary checked all those boxes. It's a unique place full of saxophones and fiery preaching and a real mix of theological views. The church has been around since the late 1800s and uses its gorgeous stained-glass windows and vaulted ceilings well, hosting everything from theatrical performances to farmers' markets to art galleries to an affordable neighborhood preschool. And it had a solid church nursery to back me up. If I was going to solo parent two young kids on Sunday mornings, that was a nonnegotiable.

In early January at Calvary, the pastor was on vacation, so a member of the church shared his testimony in lieu of the sermon. He told his personal story of growing up evangelical, of living in a black-and-white theology, of getting married and starting a family and working for a nonprofit dedicated to creating affordable housing in the city. But then he hit a wall in his early 30s; the religion that had shaped his life thus far was no longer working when he was faced with suffering.

God felt far away, he said. This early midlife crisis sent him in a downward spiral and searching for a way to rejuvenate his faith in God. He found meaning in reading Franciscan priest Richard Rohr (who my friends and I jokingly call the white Christian man whisperer). Through Rohr, he was introduced to Ignatian spirituality, which is still firmly Christian but holds a more expansive theology than most conservative evangelicals do. With Ignatian spiritual principles, he was able to pray again. I resonated with his testimony because it has been my story too.

But all of the spiritual sampling within the Christian tradition I have done in my life—grabbing some Mennonite simplicity here, sprinkling in some centering prayer there, attending Mass at the Visitation Monastery—gives me pause. Instead of digging deep into one tradition, getting down far enough to strike the water of abundant life, I have turned to a new community to start the dig all over again. I worry that the shallow soil is easier to cultivate, even if I know there will be rocks and compacted soil and maybe some buried skeletons along the way.

And now I was doing it again—attending a new church and starting a year-long spiritual formation program to become a Visitation Companion. I was chasing after the phrase "spiritual singleness," trying to find a new paradigm for understanding my faith after Josh's deconversion. Would my commitments survive the inevitable struggle to come?

For some millennials like me, especially those teetering into the post-Christian camp, delving into other Christian traditions becomes a Hail Mary (no pun intended) in an effort to hold on to faith before it dissolves completely. We are open to attending a variety of church services, exploring older Christian traditions, and drawing on spiritual practices that have been around for millennia. Like the new monastics, we are turning to faith practices that have stood the test of time, yearning for stability in a world that feels chaotic. The regularity of the liturgy is a comfort in an age when nondenominational churches seem untethered by any sense of history. Many are open to reading about the saints, dabbling with different liturgies, and looking for God in new ways. Or, as it were, old ways.

Denominational wandering is not unusual for modern Christians, nor do I think it's necessarily a bad thing. For millennials, the schisms over finer theological points, such as child versus adult baptism or what happens at Communion, matter less than the authenticity of the congregation and its activity on issues of social importance: racial justice, environmental activism, inclusion of LGTBQ people, and the like. Fewer and fewer of us are centered in just one denomination. We are spiritual explorers, looking for new ways to find God. And when the church shows its ugly underbelly, many of my generation are looking for God outside institutional religion's walls.

Postmodernism offered us a worldview with everything seen in shades of gray; we are in search of a faith that gives space for mystery, for nuance, and for evidence that God is active in the world. We want to see people walking the walk—giving away their money, advocating for low-wage workers, sheltering un-documented immigrants. I see that authenticity in how Calvary feeds homeless people every Sunday after church for a drop-in meal. I see it in the commitment the nuns have made to being good neighbors in North Minneapolis.

I may be chasing the light by attending prayer at a Catholic monastery, but I don't think God minds. God knows we need a blast of sunshine, even for just a few seconds.

10

GOOD INTENTIONS

*D*uring the second week of January, just a few weeks after that disastrous Christmas Eve at Calvary, I walked a half mile down my street to the monastery. It was the first monthly meeting of the Visitation Companions, where I had committed to join a group of laypeople to learn about Salesian spirituality. It was a frigid morning, much colder than that day in November when the words "spiritual singleness" first entered my mind. That phrase seemed to point me back toward the nuns. But could I trust it was a message from God?

I wasn't sure, but I walked to the monastery anyway.

After morning Mass concluded, I creaked down the steps into the basement room with a heavy-looking couch and chairs organized in a small circle. A group of middle-aged ladies looked over to me as I entered the room, then one motioned over to an empty spot on the couch.

"Come, sit," said a woman with snowy white hair. It was Jody, the co-coordinator of the program I had emailed back in November. "We're just about to get started."

I took my place among the small group. Salesian spirituality, I learned, was based on the spiritual writing and doctrine of Saint Francis de Sales, who happened to be the patron saint of writers and a "Doctor of the Love of God" in the Catholic Church. Saint Francis was not only a best-selling author but also a missionary to the Protestant strongholds in seventeenth-century France and, in four short years, converted a whole region back to the Catholic faith. (Not very ecumenical, I thought to myself.) Unlike some of his contemporaries, Francis's missionary tactics did not include threats or physical violence. One of his maxims was, "All through love, nothing through force."

Before we got into all that, though, we went around and introduced ourselves. One woman introduced herself as Jane, "just like Saint Jane de Chantal!" who was a cofounder of the Visitation order with Saint Francis. She explained that her daughter was starting at a Visitation Catholic school and that she was here to learn more about Salesian spirituality.

"Each school meeting begins with a prayer from Saint Francis de Sales," Jane said, passing around small sheets of papers she had brought to share. "It's called the 'Direction of Intentions.' May I read it aloud?"

We all nodded.

"My God, I give you this day," Jane read. "I offer You, now all the good that I shall do and promise to accept, for love of You, all the difficulties that I shall meet. Help me to conduct myself this day in a manner pleasing to You."

"Setting intentions is one of the core practices of Salesian spirituality," said Sister Suzanne from her blue easy chair. "Francis was a genius at sanctifying the ordinary moments of a day, and he taught people how to start each task by giving it over to God."

I shifted in my chair. Whenever I hear the word *intentions*, I can't help but think of the saying that the road to hell is paved with them. It's one thing to study an ancient form of Christian spirituality because you *intend* to grow, but it's another thing to be actually *formed*. Transformed. I suspect that Saint Francis de Sales would point me back to the ordinary moments of my day.

Setting intentions also reminds me of yoga.

Once a week, I attend a class at the YMCA. The teacher, a muscular woman with a long gray braid, welcomes me into the basement classroom. She shows me what blocks or straps I might need during the poses and where I can find a spare yoga mat from the community pile when I have forgotten mine.

"Before we get started," she says while walking barefoot around the room, sidestepping mats, "take a moment to set an intention for this practice." The room smells like rubber, like feet.

Sitting cross-legged, eyes closed, I think back to how the morning went, my flaws saturating my mental picture like a red stain: I spent too long scrolling through Instagram again, or yelled at my kids, or bought something I didn't need at Target, or thought uncharitable thoughts about the coworker who missed a deadline.

Then, in a deep awareness of my lack, I come up with some intention like "presence" or "patience." Or, just a desperate "please help."

The yoga class lasts about an hour, and I join the others who follow the movements of the instructor from mountain pose to swan diving down and up again, the group moving like a synchronized ballet company. I watch myself in the studio mirror. Standing in tree pose, I find a stationary focal point to stare at, willing myself not to wobble. I amaze myself with an ability to focus, to keep my eyes fastened on a singular point.

As I lie down for the final savasana, or corpse pose, my mind is blissfully blank, and later I walk out from the class feeling warm and loose. A twisted knot unwound. But as the day goes on and my child throws a tantrum in the YMCA lobby, or I sit in traffic on the highway, or there are no groceries in the house and I need to make dinner, the strings begin to tighten again. I forget all about my virtuous intention. Patience and presence and "please help" are all out the window.

Saint Francis de Sales did have something to say about how to set intentions that stick. His prayer of intention begins: "I offer you all the good I might do," which sounds a little like the evangelical worship songs of my youth, but then it goes on. "I promise to accept, for the love of you, all the difficulties that I meet." In a book of his letters, Saint Francis warned against idealism and overeagerness, writing that "violent effort spoils both your heart and the business at hand."

Living out one's intentions, according to de Sales, is not about trying really hard or having intense emotions but about embracing reality. Bad traffic is a reality. Small children tend to throw tantrums, and a parent should anticipate that her day will include these things. The daily chores of making meal plans and going grocery shopping are to be anticipated. How can I set an intention that allows me to accept the world as it actually is?

As the Visitation Companions meeting closed, Jody and Sister Suzanne gave each person two books on Salesian spirituality to start reading for the following month. I tucked the books under my arm for the walk home. At the intersection of Fremont and Broadway, I waited for the light to change and took several deep breaths. The bright snowbanks glittered like broken glass.

When I closed my eyes, I could see the red stain: resentment toward Josh for leaving the faith, apathy toward God, cynicism toward church.

What did I really want? Deep down, if I was truly honest, I didn't want to feel lonely in church or to embrace "spiritual singleness" or manage my kids in the fellowship hall alone. I wanted us to share the same faith again, just as I'm sure Josh wished that I had lost mine with him.

When the light turned green, I crossed the street. "God." I spoke into the cold as I walked to the other side. "God, help me find a way back to you. Help me feel less alone." As I spoke the words out loud, I realized I was setting my intention for the year of spiritual formation ahead.

11

ORCAS

A few years ago, I attended a writing workshop near Seattle. From the airport, I took a shuttle to a ferry. I rolled my suitcase out onto the deck to watch the ocean, the horizon line barely distinguishable as pale sky and pale water blended together. Salt spray tickled my nose and the cool metal railing felt slippery in my grip. I pulled out my cellphone and took a few photos—one of the water-horizon-sky and another the ship's bow, an orange life preserver fastened onto the boat's guardrail, a jot of brilliant color amid the gray-on-gray-on-gray.

Later, after I'd settled into my room in a cottage at the writers' retreat, my phone pinged. A new email popped up from an old friend, Caroline, whom I hadn't seen or talked to since we attended Honey Rock Camp together as teenagers. "Stina," she wrote. "I saw your photo of the ferry on Instagram. I live just a few miles away! Can we get coffee?" She had recognized the landscape, the ferry, the blurry horizon. I wrote her back and we set up a time to meet.

On the way home from the workshop, I took the ferry again. The week had been full, with morning sessions and afternoon sessions and evening sessions. I sat on my oversized suitcase out on the deck and stared at the water, letting my mind stretch out and race over the waves. The motor of the ferryboat rumbled, making the deck vibrate softly, and diesel fumes mixed with the scent of sea, sour with sharp. My eyes went out of focus and then I closed them, listening to the other passengers' chatter, feeling the motion of the boat beneath me.

"Look, look!" I heard someone say to my right, a little too loudly. Annoyed, I opened my eyes to squint out at the view. A cluster of people were at the ferry's guardrail, pointing out into the ocean water. My eyes followed and then I saw it. Orcas slipping in and out of the water, their backs like horseshoes, like sea snakes, like magic. I stood up and walked to the railing, pressing my body over the side to watch. Up and down, in and out, over and under. The motion was fluid, constant, large orcas and small orcas together, staying in formation. I wished for a glass-bottomed boat—or a scuba mask to wear as I plunged my face underwater to watch their full range of movement, to glimpse their white throats.

Soon, the orca pod moved to the right, getting smaller and smaller as the ferry plowed on its route. I stood and stared until I could barely distinguish their black backs from the waves.

Caroline picked me up from the ferry dock in her black Honda Pilot. We smiled and hugged and took in each other's appearance, registering the fifteen years since we last saw one another: the new smile lines on each other's faces and subtle streaks of gray hair. She led me to her car, and I hoisted my suitcase into the trunk, then settled into the front seat. Apart from the occasional Facebook post and photo, I didn't really know what was new in her life, and I was curious why she had reached out. Was it just to reminisce, or to reconnect?

"Stina, I am so glad I get to talk to you!" she said as we drove down the foggy streets toward Edmonds, the wipers swishing away the drizzle. "I've been wanting to connect with you since I read that article you wrote for *Christianity Today*. Your writing about Josh's faith loss is my story, too. But I'm the one who lost God."

I blinked back my surprise. At camp, Caroline had been "on fire" for God. One of her heroes had been Ruth Bell Graham, Billy Graham's wife, and she aspired to be just like her: faithful, steadfast, and utterly devoted to Jesus. At the time, I had been a little derisive of her love for Ruth Bell Graham. Wasn't that a bit retro? Shouldn't we be admiring women of faith who did more than support their more famous husbands—someone like Corrie ten Boom, who hid Jews in her house during World War II, or at least Elisabeth Elliot, who went back on the mission field alone after her husband was killed? In my narrow understanding, Ruth Bell Graham was the 1950s housewife of evangelicalism and, I admit, I had put Caroline in that same small box.

We drove to a little café and, over a small table, ate salmon crepes and talked about religion, marriage, and how our post-Bible camp years were cloaked with disillusionment. She told me her story about losing faith in God, of that certainty and assurance slipping through her fingers entirely, and how it impacted her husband, Jake. She could no longer hold on to her crumbling evangelical faith and found tremendous release in finally allowing herself to let go, even though it caused tension in her marriage.

"Agnosticism was sweet relief," she told me, a porcelain coffee mug cradled in her hands. "I never in a million years wanted to hurt Jake, same as I'm sure Josh never wanted to hurt you, but I was lost to myself during my deconstruction. We hate ourselves more for hurting those around us. That's why people who are losing their faith often choose not to tell others, which, of course, only increases the guilt and the loss."

I nodded, picking up my own mug to match hers, wondering if Josh felt the same way. Outside, the rain streaked down the windows.

Her eyes locked with mine. "I really scared Jake. But here is what is beautiful about our story: he stayed and loved me through it. Somehow in the midst of his wife throwing him for the biggest loop of his life, he was able to hold these opposing emotions in tandem: fear and betrayal with commitment and love."

I nodded again, remembering Jake from camp. He was a real adventurer, participating in Honey Rock Camp's five-week-long trip to the Canadian wilderness, and he always wore yellow bandanas. He and Caroline had been dating since high school and once planned to start a church together.

"How?" I asked her, pushing aside my fork. "How did Jake do that?"

She went on to tell about the hard and raw conversations they had soon after her faith deconstruction. When Caroline honestly answered Jake's questions, he would leave the room and they wouldn't speak for the rest of the afternoon. But then at night, he'd silently roll over and hug her in bed.

"I remember the first time he did this," she said, tucking a strand of hair behind her ear. "I almost revolted, saying, 'How can you touch me? Have I not pushed you away enough?' His only response was, 'Do you see whose arms are holding you? I'm here.' Jake's heart is why we made it through the roughest patch. That's the power that a spouse holds for their partner turning agnostic or atheist."

I let go of my breath, which I'd just realized I'd been holding.

"And Jake and I, well, we are a little further along in this journey than you and Josh are," she said. "When we celebrated our ten-year anniversary and decided we needed to do something big, we flew to Maine, just the two of us, and renewed our vows together. We even wrote new ones. It was the best thing we've ever done."

The hours ticked by and we sat in that café, sharing the broken fragments of the dreams we had so carelessly built up as teenagers at Bible camp, not realizing how fragile everything was. We were once so confident that our futures would be bright, that God would give us the things we wanted: strong marriages, clear vocations that made a difference in the world, strong and steady faith to weather life's storms. Yet, as I listened to Caroline talk through the painful years when God seemed absent and her marriage struggled, I felt a soft brush of hope. Somehow, they had emerged from the fires. "We are a little further along in this journey than you and Josh are," she had said. "We took our hands off each other. We let our love be free of religious conditions."

The rain was heavier when we finally left the little café. I started to pull on my raincoat, one arm at a time. "Here," Caroline said, grabbing my hand. She pulled me under her umbrella. "Let's share this." We walked over the cobblestoned sidewalk to her car, sidestepping rivulets of water.

On the drive away from the café, the rain got heavier and the windshield wipers were on overdrive. I told Caroline about seeing the orca pod, about the motion of the whales' black backs slipping in and out of water. Visible and invisible.

"No way!" she said. "I've taken that ferry hundreds of times and I've only seen orcas once. That's really special."

She turned the defrost on high and tiny circles of clear windshield blossomed upward through the fog. We sat companionably, listening to the whine from the AC and to the rain, which rang like pebbles on the car roof.

12

MY MYSTICAL SISTERS,
THE SAINTS

W hen I was looking for a new church to attend without Josh by my side, I wanted a big, diverse community to help me raise my kids in the faith. At Calvary, there are gaggles of young families and a robust children's ministry. There are parenting courses and playgroups, youth service trips and book clubs.

The only problem with moving from a teeny-tiny church to a midsized church is that it takes more time and effort to get to know people. Newcomers have to join a small group, volunteer on a committee, or regularly attend a Bible study to move relationships beyond small talk. And when there are many traditional nuclear families, it can be lonely showing up week after week solo with a couple of kids in tow. During that awkward fellowship hour after the service, I balance paper plates with pretzels, fruit, and veggies for my kids, smiling and saying hellos as I keep one eye on my three-year old, who is darting through the busy room. Hardly the environment for more than the most basic chitchat.

Each Sunday in the new church, I drop my kids in the nursery and return to the sanctuary alone. Sometimes I sit with my friends Sam and Brandi from college, but mostly I find a spot by myself, toward the back right, where the other singles go. Sometimes I watch the married couples around me: arms draped around the back of the pew, whispering to each other during announcements, passing a baby back and forth.

I am used to it by now; it's been four years since Josh and I regularly sat in church together. But then some moments catch me off-guard: a married couple stands up front and presents their baby for dedication, a dad stands up and asks for prayer for his college-aged son. Waves of loss hit me all over again—*we* used to be that couple dedicating a baby; *he* used to ask the congregation for prayer when family members hit hard times.

I look at the other people sitting in pews alone and wonder if they ever feel lonely in a church filled with families. In the Catholic Church, singleness is required for priests, monks, and nuns, though I am sure many unmarried lay Catholics feel the sting of exclusion in their parishes.

Lately, as I read about the saints in my Catholic prayer book, I imagine them showing up for church with me. I see Saint Jane de Chantal with her rounded black veil from the 1600s as she slides into the empty space next to me in the pew. Saint Margaret Mary, blissed out after a mystical union with God, wedges next to her, her eyes closed during the sermon. I spot Elisabeth Leseur in the balcony, where she is privately reading a book of theology. Up ahead, Saint Monica raises her hands in worship while tears drip down her face. I see them shifting in their seats; I imagine them seeing me and nodding.

I nod back at these women, joining their communion, the sisterhood of the single or spiritually single, the long legacy of empowered women who embrace their faith no matter what obstacles are thrown at them. When I learn about their lives, I don't feel so lonely. I imagine them all around me, that great cloud of witnesses, and I am ready for the next step.

Some might say these female saints are all married to Jesus. Well, technically all Christians are part of the church, which is described by the Apostle Paul as God's bride. But is there a special relationship between those of us who are spiritually single—the ones with no earthly spiritual spouse? Are our friendships with one another stronger? Are we mystical siblings to one another? Certainly the relationship between committed celibate people—the sisters who have lived in community with one another for decades—is unique. Are there special relationships for the married but spiritually single as well?

I like this idea of a mystical sisterhood extending backward through time and space. My fellow females who are, at the very least, devoted to Jesus, lend me an example of what it looks like to love, serve, and follow God.

Sainthood is a slippery thing. It's easy to deify people who have led remarkable lives, especially when a century or more has gone by and all that glorious human complexity has been smoothed over or lost. Sometimes I read about the miracles these women performed in the fourth century and think, *yeah right.* I read about the impossibly pious nun who gave away all her money and kissed all the lepers and think, *why even try?*

In Robert Ellsberg's book, *Blessed Among All Women: Women Saints, Prophets, and Witnesses for Our Time,* he includes biographies of famous saints like Joan of Arc and Hildegard of Bingen and also impressive women outside the Catholic tradition. The modern women featured in the collection aren't the type who run off and join (or establish) a monastery but instead "find God in the realm of work, family, community, and the ordinary business of life." These ordinary saints leave "no monument in the world" but contribute to the world's growing goodness. These kinds of quiet role models live the vocation of the greatest saints: "to embrace God's love and reflect it back to the world."

A faithful, hidden life. That is a sainthood I understand. It's a sainthood I see all around me; in every church and school and community center I have ever attended, there are dozens of regular, quietly faithful people. And it's a sainthood that is well known by many women who have traditionally raised children, cared for elders, and held the fabric of society together while men have been off doing other things.

So why write about Catholic saints when there are plenty of women in my own Protestant tradition to exemplify? Why take the time to explore their lives? Maybe it's because I'm lonely in a church filled with nuclear families and am looking for companions who understand spiritual singleness. Maybe it's because I see their example and know that the obstacles in my life are not unusual, that I can carry on and serve God with my life despite my struggles.

Ellsberg writes that the "story of each holy person is also a story about God." I suppose that's the other answer—that I can't find God, and the saints tell me to keep looking.

13

January 23

SAINT JANE

When Mother Teresa's private letters and other writings were published posthumously in 2009, many were shocked by the deep spiritual struggle she—a saint—experienced. For years, she was desolate and felt God's absence. She wrote: "If I ever become a Saint—I will surely be one of 'darkness.'"

Like Mother Teresa, Saint Jane de Chantal wrestled with intense spiritual torments. She is famous for cofounding the Visitation order with Saint Francis de Sales, and her picture is up all over the Visitation Monastery down the street. The biographies all claim that Jane had a happy marriage, though they also say there were seven pregnancies in eight years, and three of the babies died in infancy. The biographies also say that Jane's husband was unfaithful to her, and she raised a child he fathered with another woman.

A happy marriage? Perhaps the standards were different in the seventeenth century.

In any case, Jane loved her husband. When he was killed in a hunting accident, Jane harbored rage and bitterness for years toward the man who accidentally shot her husband.

Another tidbit from the biographies—Jane was a shrewd business manager who provided for the poor. After her husband's death, Jane's father-in-law commandeered her and threatened to disinherit her children unless she managed his estate and helped raise his illegitimate offspring. Not a happy decade for her after her husband's death—no wonder she spent those years twisted by sorrow, unwilling to forgive the man who killed her husband. She vowed never to marry again.

Jane, from the beginning, wanted a deeper relationship with God, but she struggled with forgiveness. Four years after her husband's death, she heard a sermon preached by Francis de Sales, then the bishop of Geneva. Hearing Francis's sermon was a turning point for Jane. She connected with his message—that all people are loved by God and called to live a holy life, even widows with children like herself. Jane reached out to Francis to ask if he would be her spiritual director, and Francis agreed to take Jane on. It was after meeting Francis that Jane was able to let go of the resentment she felt toward her husband's killer and embrace a new calling in her life.

Jane and Francis had a remarkable relationship. In the introduction to a collection of their letters, Henri Nouwen wrote about what a special, Christ-centered, spiritual friendship the two of them modeled. Historically, Jane is depicted as the mentee, the female under the great care and leadership of Francis. But in their letters to one another, it becomes clear that they mutually influenced one another. Jane's strong business acumen shines through, as well as her experience mothering and living for God within the confines of her familial obligations.

Originally Francis and Jane had wanted to establish a monastic community that was not enclosed, allowing the women to freely visit with the poor and needy without the separation of a cloister. Their vision for the religious order was to create a community for women who could not handle the rigor of ascetic orders that demand long hours of prayer on one's knees. They wanted to welcome older women, the infirm, widows, or others who would be rejected from religious life. If all are called to holiness, they reasoned, what about women like Jane—in her 30s, widowed, a mother of four children? At that time, no other monastic community would grant entrance to a woman like her.

Francis and Jane had a special bond, and their letters to each other show an intense intimacy. Together they popularized a radical new philosophy of Christian spirituality that focused deeply on a universal call to holiness.

Jane had other spiritual friends, including Saint Vincent de Paul (founder of the Daughters of Charity). Upon Jane's death, de Paul wrote: "She was full of faith, yet all her life had been tormented by thoughts against it." Her faith impressed him because she faced the challenge of intense doubts, of intrusive thoughts that went against everything she worked for in her life, yet she continued walking in faith.

Jane continued on after Francis's death, even after several of her adult children died and the Black Plague claimed many lives in her community. Some biographers wonder if she suffered from clinical depression in her later years. There is no denying that she was good at her work. When she died at age sixty-nine, there were some eighty-five autonomous Visitation monasteries, and she helped start them all.

When I show up at Calvary and find my spot toward the back, I sometimes see Jane in the pew ahead of me adjusting her long, black habit. During prayers I peek at her to see if her face betrays any sign of inner torment, but her face is slack and serene. Later, during the fellowship hour, I catch her slipping away through the back door. She must be getting back to her work, back to all that God has impressed on her to do.

Saint Jane had intense doubts, I know, yet she was also full of faith. It is paradoxical, and a little annoying. Jane was a mother, like me, juggling childcare and back-to-school nights and balancing the checkbook. She harbored resentment for many years toward the man who accidentally shot her husband. She embodies something her pal Saint Francis de Sales once wrote her: "I am as human as anyone could possibly be."

Her imperfection makes her someone I can learn from. It's from the real, human saints like Jane that we learn what holiness looks like "in the choices they made; in their struggles to be faithful, even in the face of doubts and disappointments; in their everyday victories over pride and selfishness; in their daily efforts to be more truthful, loving, and brave."

Jane, too, was "spiritually single." She was a foundress, a widow, a mother, and yet a profoundly real woman who evidently battled with her physical and mental health at times.

She, like me, struggled with resentment. And still the Catholic Church considers her a saint.

It isn't lost on me that Jane suffered from painful spiritual aridity—something I can relate to in this season of my life. But when I read her letters, I see an intimacy and openness. Despite her doubts, Jane made it a point to find spiritual companions for the journey. It was once she befriended Francis that she was able to forgive the past and embrace a new calling in her life.

14

DISCERNING THE WAY
YOU SHOULD GO

*O*ne snowy January night, I walked up the steps to the Saint Jane House for a gathering the nuns were hosting on the topic of discernment. The Saint Jane House is named, you guessed it, after foundress Jane de Chantal, and it's a place of hospitality affiliated with the Visitation Sisters. I decided to attend the four-part series not because I had a major life decision to make but because I was eager to spend more time with the sisters.

What I didn't realize was that evening would lead me to question whether I should have gotten married in the first place.

Inside, I removed my snow boots and put on the complimentary slippers provided for each guest, taking in the cozy scene: a fire in the fireplace, comfortable looking couches and stuffed chairs arranged in a circle in the living room, candles flickering on the coffee table and mantel, and Sister Karen walking over to greet me.

"Stina!" she said. "I am so glad you could make it." She ushered me over to the hall closet so I could hang up my coat, then to the dining room table where I signed in, wrote my name on a nametag, and gathered the handouts.

"Grab yourself a mug of tea or coffee and find a place in the circle," Sister Karen told me. "We are going to get started soon."

I wandered over to the kitchen and found an earthenware mug with the words "Be who you are and be that well" etched on the side. Later I would learn that those were the words of Saint Francis de Sales, a reflection on his belief that anyone can imitate Jesus in his or her particular season of life.

After a moment of silence, an opening prayer, and group introductions, Sister Katherine spoke about the series on discernment, explaining that at each session one person would share his or her story of making an important life decision.

When Sister Katherine told her vocation story, she described how her parents made her go to college, even though she would much rather have joined the convent right out of high school. Wisely, her parents cautioned her against making such a huge life decision at age eighteen. They encouraged her to go out into the world first. Sister Katherine's desire—one might say calling—was so strong that even in college she felt the tug to join. She met with a Dominican priest to talk through her predicament. Should she stay and finish college or begin her novitiate right away? The priest then did something she did not expect.

He took out a coin and said, "Heads, you finish college, tails, you join the convent now."

Katherine was aghast. Why would the priest do such a thing? Who dares to flip a coin to decide the future? But then the priest went ahead and flicked the coin in the air where it soared, then tumbled. Katherine didn't look at the coin.

"I know what I want. I want to join the convent now."

The priest smiled. "You knew all along what the right decision was. The coin was just a way to force your hand, to reveal what you really knew deep inside."

In Salesian spirituality, Sister Katherine went on to explain, this freedom is called "liberty of spirit." It gives credence to one's own will and desires, suggesting that those things are often indications of God's guidance (as long as they don't contradict God's "declared will" as found in Christian doctrine and Scripture). We can often trust our own hearts to know what God wants for us, which is to be happy and whole.

This idea seemed radical to me. I was formed spiritually in evangelical institutions, which emphasized humankind's total depravity. How can we trust ourselves if we are inherently sinful? How can we possibly make good or right decisions when our judgement is constantly muddied by our unholy thoughts, our incorrect actions?

In truth, these two concepts are not at odds with each other—sin is real yet our natural desires are not always wrong or bad. A healthy spirituality doesn't discount desire *or* sin. In my own experience, I had an unhealthy propensity to question every decision, to view God's will as a black-and-white journey that you either follow perfectly or not at all.

After Sister Katherine shared her story, the nuns instructed us to break into small groups. We went around the room and counted off, round robin, and soon we gathered into groups of four. My small group gathered on the couch nearest to the fire. A woman in her midfifties introduced herself.

"The story honestly made me sad," she said. "I just got divorced after spending two decades of my life married to someone I shouldn't have married in the first place." She grabbed a tissue from the coffee table. Sister Katherine patted her back sympathetically.

"When we were first dating," she said, "I knew that God was telling me not to marry him, but I did anyway because I wanted to. I didn't wait and listen. I was wrong and I missed it; I missed what my life was supposed to be about."

We sat there for a moment, letting her lament take shape in the air around us. I shifted in my seat, trying to get comfortable. Another man in our small group spoke about his divorce, how it had totally altered his life. But he said that he couldn't view it as a mistake, that he wouldn't be the person he is now without the journey he had taken.

The fireplace was putting out a lot of heat, and I was starting to sweat. Maybe attending a discernment group full of recently divorced people had been a mistake. Was this my future? What if the warnings were true, that if we weren't aligned spiritually, nothing would work? Would I be here in my fifties, lamenting my decades of marriage to Josh?

In our small group, Sister Katherine talked about how, even after deciding to join the convent, she had struggled. She had suffered from scruples—which I had never heard of before. It's a tendency to become overly introspective, weighing each individual action looking for flaws, paralyzed by fear of doing the wrong thing. She said this affliction tormented her—this gnawing, accusatory inner voice, calling out each and every imperfection. Even after saying yes to religious life, she had to grow and learn to experience the love and grace of God. "It was a trust issue," she told us.

Plenty of young women who, like Sister Katherine, joined convents at age nineteen didn't end up living the next sixty years in monastic communities. The kind of religious life that Katherine entered in the 1950s doesn't exist anymore. As a novice, she was cloistered away from the outside world, shedding street clothes and adopting a habit, no longer able to leave and visit family for birthdays, holidays, or even funerals. Doctors and dentists would come into the convent to treat the sisters so they didn't have to leave the cloister. She even took a new name when she entered the convent, becoming Sister Mary William. The changes to religious life after the Second Vatican Council in the early 1960s were extreme for many: Catholic sisters reevaluated medieval rules that stipulated the length of their habit, and many religious orders (like the Visitation Sisters) stopped requiring them at all. Nuns could hold onto their birth names. Conflicts broke out in convents around the world over reforming the liturgies, altering ascetic practices, and even attending college far from the motherhouse. Many sisters left.

My friend Susan said recently that most people romanticize nuns to the point of dehumanization. Even though all Christians are called to be holy, we still place religious types on pedestals, imagining them to be closer to God than the rest of us. Most nuns have the advantage of a structured, external rhythm of prayer, and no doubt these rhythms have done much to cultivate an interior life devoted to God. But nuns, just like the saints, are humans, too.

Would Sister Katherine have jumped at the chance to join the convent at nineteen if she had known so much would change—both in herself and in the institution that she had committed to? Did her scruples cause her to question her decision to become a nun? It couldn't have been easy to stay, to continue choosing to be a nun, when others walked away.

I asked her that question one day.

"No, I don't regret it," she said. "My heart knew."

Sister Katherine knew what she desired, so she left college to join the enclosed community at age nineteen. What a risky, audacious thing—to trust one's adolescent self enough to make a lifelong commitment. What a risky, audacious thing for any married couple to pledge themselves to each other for life, not knowing how they might change or who they would become in a decade.

When Josh first lost his religion, I looked back to our wedding day with an accusatory glare. This was not what I signed up for. We were twenty when we met, twenty-five when we made those lifelong vows to each other, come what may. Did I believe that God was guiding me to marry Josh? Could I trust my own desires at that young age as being within God's will? Should we have even gotten married in the first place?

Discernment always involves risk, no matter how judiciously we weigh the pros or cons. And, Saint Francis de Sales writes, Christians live somewhere between God's two wills: God's "declared will" in Scripture and Christian tradition, and the "will of God's good pleasure" where we practice freedom to follow our intuition. There is a creative, healthy tension by living between those wills, Sister Katherine claimed. And, once we have prayerfully discerned something, we shouldn't indulge our scruples by doubting the choices we make.

Did God lead me to marry Josh, even though it means I am now in a "spiritually single" marriage? I can't be sure. All I know is that, like Sister Katherine, I don't regret it. I love this man who sincerely wrestled with his faith and, when he stopped believing, had the courage to walk away, despite the cost. My heart knew then, and still does now.

15

THE LITTLE VIRTUES

*T*o become a Visitation Companion, I pledged to attend monthly spiritual formation meetings at the monastery. Together with a small group of laywomen, we read the writings of Saints Francis and Jane and, after Mass, navigated the steep steps down to the monastery's basement for discussion with our leaders Jody and Sister Suzanne. At the end of the year, during Advent, the individuals in our small group would discern whether we should become Companions to the monastery, partnering with the sisters in their ministry.

And so, on a Wednesday morning in February, I found myself on a sagging couch sitting next to Kristin and Kathie, holding a calligraphic design of something called "The Little Virtues." On the badly photocopied page, letters crept upward and around, amassing into a giant ball. They formed ornately written words like *humility, gentleness,* and *patience.*

Our leader Jody explained that when Francis and Jane were shaping the Visitation order, they chose these little virtues to emphasize as they decided on their rule of life and battled with the authorities to allow women to live a semicloistered life in the community (a battle they ultimately lost). After taking a sip from my paper cup of coffee, I read the list and bristled: be grateful, be cheerfully optimistic, be kind.

If anything, I thought, I need a spirituality that encourages me to be assertive, bold, and unafraid of what others think about me. I need to cultivate courage and strength and follow-through. When our spiritual formation group discussed the little virtues that morning in the monastery's basement, I confessed my discomfort.

"I don't want to make myself cheerfully optimistic about my marriage right now," I said, pointing to the handout. Kristin, who sat beside me on the couch, nodded. We had all shared deeply about our personal lives already. "I get why it's important to be kind and gentle, but what I really want is to be brave. Why isn't that on here?"

Sister Suzanne interjected that the opportunity for big virtues—bravery, boldness, prophetic imagination—generally comes around only a handful of times in a typical person's life. Many of us spend more time washing dishes or going to work in an office than leading revolutions or being arrested for civil disobedience. Saint Francis believed in the holiness of all people (a sort of Catholic expression of the priesthood of all believers) at a time when holiness was reserved for the most devout and ascetic practices of the professional religious: monks, nuns, and priests. Elevating the little virtues—honesty, generosity, thoughtful concern for others—meant affirming the holiness in every person, who has the opportunity to practice such virtue every day, multiple times, in multiple ways.

When I told Sister Brenda about my negative reaction to the little virtues, she surprised me by asking: "I wonder what is really behind your reaction? The practice of the little virtues is meant to shape our inner life to be more like Jesus. There is nothing wrong with cultivating true humility."

Indeed. The little virtues did bring up a caricature of a long-suffering, meek Christian woman for me instead of shining a path to everyday holiness as they were intended. I wasn't sure why.

Maybe it was because the virtues seemed retrograde to me, like the black-and-white photo in a book about the St. Paul Visitation Monastery I found recently, which showed a nun in a full habit instructing teenage women in Twiggy 1960s hairdos about proper table manners. The book described how the first Visitation Monastery in Minnesota was started back in the late 1800s when wealthy Catholic families bankrolled a new convent. Their patrons included railroad tycoon James J. Hill, whose mansion in St. Paul is sometimes referred to as "Minnesota's Downton Abbey." The Catholic elite in the new industrial city wanted a finishing school for their girls, and the Visitation Sisters had experience running such schools. The all-girls high school, which offered both boarding and nonboarding options, was to impart academic rigor as well as virtue in the lives of these wealthy young women. Notably, Mollie McQuillan Fitzgerald, the mother of F. Scott Fitzgerald, was among its graduates.

All this history reeks of classism and patriarchy. Even the orders of nuns themselves had distinctions between the sisters—some spent their time doing menial chores (cleaning, cooking, running errands, etc.) while others held higher rank. The 1600s European feudal system of patron and servant had certainly left its fingerprints all over the Visitation history. Reading about the little virtues left me wondering if this kind of theology was more about upholding hierarchical systems than acting like Jesus.

Sister Brenda reminded me of one of Saint Francis's maxims: "there is nothing so strong as gentleness, nothing so gentle as true strength." Though counterintuitive, my experience with the Visitation Sisters so far confirmed this. The sisters founded their monastery in North Minneapolis thirty years ago to "take Visitation to the poor." Sister Karen told me she was inspired by changes in the Catholic Church during the 1970s and '80s, when liberation theologians declared that God has a "preferential option" for those in poverty. This emphasis seemed to directly contradict the mission of the Visitation convents running schools that taught mostly upper-class girls. After years of prayer, the sisters forged a new path by establishing a monastic community that better embodied Francis and Jane's original vision: that the sisters be semicloistered and go out to serve their neighbor.

Yes, the sisters practiced the little virtues. They radiated with warmth and hospitality; they modeled active listening and gentleness. But there was also a steely strength underneath those softer virtues, a formidable resolve and healthy boundaries. These are women who don't wear makeup, who wear sensible shoes, and who open their shared housing to people experiencing homelessness. Many have lived their entire adult lives in a community of other women, never relying solely on men to move their furniture or fix the jiggly door handle. They are organized and persistent, having endured decades of common life in community pre- and post-Vatican II. They are neither passive nor timid, remaining faithful to their vows. They are the hearty ones who have stayed in the church amid decline, who have seen their traditions devalued and mocked, who devote their lives to singing the Psalms and embracing vows of poverty, chastity, and obedience.

We all need spiritual women to live big virtues by standing in solidarity with the vulnerable and change systems that harm people. (Sister Mary Margaret does this at the Visitation Monastery by hosting a twelve-step program for reckoning with white privilege.) And we all need spiritual women who are kind, patient, and steadfast in the day-to-day small tasks that need to get done. My friend Christiana likes to remind me that when Jesus said to love your neighbor, that includes your family.

Gentleness. Patience. Kindness. Putting others before myself. Showing appreciation for Josh, who has always affirmed my commitment to take our kids to church, even though it's hard for him. How much easier it is for me to daydream about great deeds, to downgrade my ordinary life by comparing it to Dorothy Day and Mother Teresa, or to the women saints I read about each day. To imagine the ways we could be serving our neighbors if only Josh and I had stayed at Jubilee Partners, if we were both still Christians.

If Francis de Sales is right, then I am just as holy living in a mixed-faith marriage than in one where both spouses believe in God. I am holy in my everyday life as I practice virtues of patience with my children, kindness to my husband, and even gentleness with myself when I fail. When I look to my mystical sisters, I hope I can emulate their big virtues when opportunity arises: to speak out again racism in the systems I benefit from and in my own heart, to support activists on the frontlines with my money and my prayers, to be brave in living out my faith even while Josh sits on the sidelines. These ordinary saints are washing the dishes and leading the revolution, and I belong in their communion.

Long after we wrapped up our February gathering of Visitation Companions, I arrived at an answer to Sister Brenda's question. The real reason that the little virtues bothered me was because they poked at my illusions of boldly "doing great things for God." Instead, the little virtues told me to move along the laundry, to pause and delight at my son's nonsensical joke, to stay at the table and have hard conversations with Josh even when I'd rather bolt. They asked me to pay attention and be present to my actual life.

16

FELLOW PILGRIMS

$\mathcal{B}$ ack when Josh and I were dating, back when my Christian faith felt more secure, I went on a spiritual pilgrimage.

I had assumed that other pilgrims along the five-hundred-mile Camino de Santiago in northern Spain would be fellow Christians, but in most cases, they were people in the middle of an "Eat, Pray, Love"–type crisis. One blonde Canadian woman I met along the trail had recently divorced, quit her job, and sold her house. Another fiftysomething couple had lost their eldest son to suicide the year before.

To be sure, the Camino is a religious pilgrimage and officially recognized by the Roman Catholic Church. All pilgrims who can vouch that their travels are in part spiritually motivated may receive an indulgenced certificate of completion called a "compostela" once they reach Santiago. But my motivation for walking the Camino was less about sanctification and more about having a post-college adventure.

My companion on the Camino was Rachel. She was my sister Sarah's roommate from college. Sarah was newly married and pregnant with her first baby, and I suspect the email updates we sent from our internet hostels along the journey made her twinge with envy as she picked out onesies and crib sheets in suburban Virginia. We didn't have smartphones (this was 2007), so we relied on payphones or desktop computers with sticky keys in the community rooms of hostels, or tiny internet cafés where you paid Euros for fifteen-minute increments of connection.

The trail was marked by bright yellow arrows spray painted on pavement, or on boulders, or on wooden signs nailed to trees. Some days we walked on suburban sidewalks. On others we walked through dramatic fields of red tulips and up winding mountain trails, or sometimes through tiny Spanish villages where old men in tweed jackets stood in doorways of stone houses and watched us walk by. We hiked through herds of sheep, through acres of vineyards, or through noisy city traffic. Over nearly thirty days, we covered the five hundred miles of the trail without a map, the right direction obvious in bright yellow marks.

After a few hours of hiking each morning we would break for lunch, usually for a baguette and cheese, sometimes grapes or wrinkled apples we had bought from a shoebox grocery the day before. We would keep walking until we made our destination for the evening, checking into *albergues* especially for pilgrims along the Camino that stamped our passports with the name of the town. After dumping our bags and taking showers, I would meet Rachel in the albergue courtyard, each of us wearing our only pair of clean town clothes and Chaco sandals, which revealed bandaged heels and browning toenails. We joked that you could always identify another pilgrim in town because they walked with a particular limp or shuffled their legs, sore from walking ten to twenty miles a day.

Walking the Camino was the first time I participated in a spiritual practice with people outside my faith tradition. We walked together and drank from the same ancient water fountains and traded tips on blister care, yet our collective religious beliefs ranged from conservative evangelical to devout Catholic to pagan to none. Hearing these fellow pilgrims talk about their views on reincarnation felt vaguely threatening; I felt enormous pressure to share the Gospel.

I always carried my Bible with me then. It slid into my purse and had a battered, duct-taped cover. I was proud of this Bible, the way the wear and tear on its binding and pages reflected my piety. In those days, I also carried the Book of Common Prayer and a Celtic prayer book from Iona. I would find a shady table in the hostel's courtyard and open up my devotional materials, looking up the appropriate verses from the daily lectionary, praying "Christ before me, Christ behind me, Christ above me, Christ below me."

"Are you actually reading a Bible?" a fellow pilgrim asked me one day after a long day of hiking. He was a thirtyish French man who wore a red scarf jauntily around his neck. Rumor had it that he'd had several romantic relationships with pilgrims along the journey, carrying on with one woman from Pamplona to Los Arcos, then breaking it off and finding a new girlfriend by Najera. Men like this made me supremely uncomfortable with their sophisticated, women-wise ways. I was a rigid twenty-three-year-old virgin who read her Bible every morning. I was also concerned that he hadn't heard the truth about Jesus, that his soul was in danger.

"Yes, it's a Bible," I said, picking up the book to show him the binding. "Haven't you ever read one?"

"No," he said, sitting down in the wrought iron patio chair beside me. He adjusted his round spectacles, which reminded me of John Lennon. I prayed a silent prayer, wondering how I could succinctly explain the gospel message to this attractive, hedonistic French man.

I don't remember the rest of our conversation. I imagine that I fumbled through the basics: the incarnation, Jesus's crucifixion conquering death, how God was bringing a new kingdom in and through God's people. I imagine that this French man leaned in, taking in this young American woman with a blue bandana in her hair, clutching a duct-taped Bible to her chest as she talked a little too quickly. It was one of my first experiences evangelizing a truly secular person, who lived his life outside of the story of God's now-not-yet redemption for the world. These conversations made me afraid. I wanted people to know Jesus; I wanted them to be saved. But even as I spoke, the Christian words felt forced.

The conversion attempt likely ended when my friend Rachel joined us at the table, and the conversation shifted from the incarnation to which tapas restaurant we would try that evening. Rachel had just finished a year of service at the Youth with a Mission (YWAM) base in Amsterdam; her relational philosophy of evangelism was summed up by "people are not projects" and it was the Holy Spirit, not us, who changed hearts. She didn't seem to have any of my nervous energy around relating to religious outsiders.

We both had plenty of opportunities to talk about our faith along the Camino with fellow pilgrims. Many longed for transcendence; many hoped the month-long pilgrimage would somehow change their life. Yet most were the spiritual-but-not-religious, trading the pilgrim destinations of shrines and Catholic churches containing the ancient bones of saints for beer gardens and bars along the journey.

Even I was unnerved by the ornate Catholicism at every turn: gothic cathedrals, the paintings of Saint Sebastian's bloody body punctured by arrows, the altars piled with plastic figurines of baby Jesus. I couldn't help feeling like a throwback, an American evangelical in a sea of European pilgrims who had shed their Christian devotion generations ago, along with customs like bloodletting. And, as far as I know, my words and witness, my daily Bible reading and silent prayers didn't convert anyone on that trip.

I think about the Camino sometimes now when I try to incorporate spiritual practices into my marriage and family life. Sometimes I still feel like the ridiculous Christian trying to explain the tenets of faith to our kids. When I see them through Josh's eyes, they seem ludicrous.

But even if Josh and I don't share the same religion, we are still fellow pilgrims walking side by side. We are traveling through life together as we raise our kids and welcome friends into our home and struggle to define and live out our common values.

Nowadays, the only Christian practice we—irregularly—do together is the examen prayer. Josh and I first learned of examen, which Saint Ignatius of Loyola deemed the most important of daily spiritual exercises, when we attended a church small group together while we were dating. The traditional examen includes a five-step process: express gratitude for the day's blessings, invite the Holy Spirit to be present, identify missteps and faults from the day, ask for forgiveness, and ask God for help in the future.

But when Josh and I remember to pray the examen after the kids are in bed, we don't actually close our eyes and pray out loud. What we do is ask each other two simple questions: Where did you give or receive the most love today? and Where did you give or receive the least love today?

We have carried the tradition to our supper table most nights, where the kids join in the practice. We ask each other, Where did you experience love or joy today? Where did you not? It's a variation on the questions we answered during our family Advent devotions.

Invariably, I learn something about Josh that I didn't know: how, in his middle school science class that day, one of his students told him his dad just died, or that he discovered a new running trail he loves. Especially on the nights when we're fighting, or disconnected, practicing the examen forces us to lean in a little, make eye contact, and share something that impacted us that day. The practice may be the brainchild of Saint Ignatius, who himself took a famous pilgrimage to Jerusalem, but its wisdom works just as well in our agnostic-Christian home.

On the Camino, I saw people participating in spiritual practices together all the time, whether they believed in God or not. I am sure that many of those travelers had an experience with the Divine along the way, and I certainly felt bonded to the fellow pilgrims who suffered through blisters and uncomfortable hostel beds alongside me.

We were all on the trail together. Some days I would walk with one set of travelers, only to have to split up due to an injury or need for a rest day. Then, a week later, I might run into the same group at a café midmorning, and we would hug and kiss the sides of each other's cheeks like long-lost family members.

There is a famous line of poetry about spiritual pilgrimage, that "the way is made by walking." In many ways that's what Josh and I are doing in our mixed-faith marriage: making our own trail, walking together, sometimes losing each other for days. Inevitably, we find each other again, and when we do, we hug and kiss each other's cheeks. We hold on tight, then let each other go before we start out again on the trail.

17

RELINQUISHMENT

*R*elinquish:
   transitive verb

   1: to withdraw or retreat from : leave behind

   2: GIVE UP, *relinquish* a title

   3 a: to stop holding physically : RELEASE, slowly *relinquished* his grip on the bar

     b: to give over possession or control of : YIELD, few leaders willingly *relinquish* power

The thing about blazing a new trail in your interfaith home is that it costs something. The path is arduous, and no one has cleared the downed trees. There are no obvious faith practices to mutually draw from; instead, you must decide on family rhythms as you go. Advent rituals can be fraught. Praying before meals can get complicated. Even when you do the hard work of having these conversations with your partner outright, of deciding together how to handle Sunday mornings or bedtime prayers, things can unexpectedly snag.

It doesn't help that grief around Josh's deconversion can still hit me unaware. Little things can trigger it, like when I find myself crying in church during a baby dedication, or when I watched, arms crossed, as Josh cleared out his shelf of theological books and stuck them in a donation box. Or when I found a stack of old letters from college in the basement that Josh had filled with quotes from Henri Nouwen and the Psalms.

My friend Kelley says that God is teaching me something about relinquishment through all of this. When I give Josh's lack of faith over to God during moments of sadness or disappointment, I am showing great trust in God's goodness. Just keep handing him over, she tells me. Release him to God.

Her words reminded me of my conversation with Caroline a few years ago in Seattle, when I saw the pod of orcas and she told me that she and her husband had decided to "take our hands off each other." It's a curious statement. How can you be intimate with your partner if you are not touching? I want the intimacy, the trust, the interdependence. How can I do that if my hands are not on my husband, if I am not extending my arms outward to him? But I don't think that is how she meant it; I think she meant that they fully relinquished each other. They took their hands off each other in an act of unconditional love. They let their love be free of religious conditions.

Relinquishment is a practice some Christians observe during Lent, the forty days before Easter resurrection. On Ash Wednesday, the very beginning of the Lenten season, Christians are invited to repentance. It is a time to fast from something: chocolate, coffee, watching reruns of *The Office*. These small acts of self-denial are an outward sign of an inward reality, or so the pastors tell me. They mark the forty days leading up to Easter as a time of preparation, of self-examination, of getting ready for Holy Week.

"What are you giving up for Lent?" the conversation would go in the campus cafeteria back in college, usually a week before Ash Wednesday. In those days I attended an Anglican church that introduced me to joyful liturgy, Communion every Sunday, and colors for liturgical seasons: purple for Lent and Advent, green for Epiphany and ordinary time, red for Holy Week and Pentecost, and white for the biggest of celebrations: Easter and Christmas. What a novel idea, this whole church calendar thing. It felt good to give something up for a season, to let go of a habit, a food group, a small comfort in an effort to reorient my day-to-day living toward God.

Despite my good faith efforts, I've never been very good at Lent. Despite my good intentions, I often abandon my fast halfway through.

When Ash Wednesday fell on Valentine's Day this year, I had to laugh at the irony of it. It's one thing to give up chocolate or caffeine. But it's another to relinquish the love of your life, your husband, to God. I didn't want to let the picture of my marriage, my family life, die, return to the earth, and be released so it can be formed into something new.

When I join the sisters for prayer in the small chapel at the Visitation Monastery, the alleluias are noticeably gone from the liturgy and songs. There are special Lenten antiphons, and the altar is covered in purple cloth. The ascetic practices are communal, the emphasis on our corporate journey rather than my own individual failings to stick with whatever fast I've chosen.

Relinquishment is something the sisters know beyond the practice of Lent. They hold no personal property; they take vows of poverty, chastity, and obedience. They give up the autonomy that is so prized in our modern American culture; their way of life so counter to our idols of the independent woman.

But the lives the sisters lead—the people they minister to, the presence they bring to the neighborhood—wouldn't be possible without relinquishment, without vows, without remaining faithful to radical promises. Religious life looks so different than it did when many of them joined as young women, back when Visitation Sisters wore habits and recited liturgies in Latin. I wonder if that change was ever painful.

There are more nuns over the age of ninety than are under the age of sixty. Some religious communities of women are literally dying out, and with them centuries of communal practice. Sister Katherine is in charge of vocations at the Visitation Monastery; she is the first point of contact for women who are exploring their call to religious life. In all the years she has spent in this role, she has not formally recruited anyone to join their community. It can be discouraging.

Like most people as they get older, Catholic sisters are concerned about legacy—about how their communities will change as their numbers dwindle to a fraction of their former size. If the trends toward religious disaffiliation and secularization continue, the losses are felt in the broader church as well, as congregations sell their buildings and seminaries close.

My friend Amy is preparing to be ordained a priest in the Episcopal church. She is joining the ranks of ordained leadership at a time when the church is contracting, and she knows that part of her role will be to help congregations die out.

"How do I love a dying thing?" she asked me recently.

One afternoon in mid-March, I walked over to the Fremont Avenue house for midday prayer. A sign in the window was not encouraging. It read: "The sisters are not available today. Please come back at another time." Still, I rang the bell and waited for a few minutes, then pulled out my phone to check the monastery's website to see if, indeed, there was prayer today. The Visitation Monastery is housed in two separate houses, so I wondered then if I had come to the wrong one.

The day was unusually warm for March—in the forties—and I didn't mind the walk over a block to Girard Avenue to check if prayer was there instead. After what has felt like weeks of gray skies and cold, bitter weather, a sunny walk in warm temperatures can feel like a little miracle. I walked over and rang the bell to the Girard Monastery, wondering again if I had the time wrong, or if anyone was there. After a minute, I saw the shadow of someone moving behind the door's window. Sister Karen's gray bob emerged from behind the pane, and I caught her broad smile. "Stina," she said in her raspy voice. "So glad you are here." I apologized for being late and explained I'd gone to the wrong house, but she waved away my words. "Come and join us upstairs." I turned and hung up my coat and unlaced my boots, and when I turned, she was gone. Was she upstairs? I had never been in that chapel before.

I climbed the wooden steps beside an elegant banister. A metal pipe with a grooved interior was fastened to the wall beside the railing—a track for a chair to move its way up and down the stairway for the most elderly sisters who could no longer navigate the steps. At the top of the landing I looked around at a variety of doors that were open, trying to locate where the chapel was. "In here," I heard, so I followed the voice into a carpeted space with six chairs. Two chairs were vacant, and I hesitated until Sister Karen patted the seat beside herself. "Here," she said. The other nuns smiled at me as I settled in, peering at the altar that held images of Mary, mother of God, in paintings and sculpture forms. There was a tiny wardrobe of sorts, with a keyhole in its front door, perched on top of the altar, and I wondered if it was the tabernacle where they kept the consecrated host, the sacred body of Christ.

"We are using a special antiphon today for Lent, so just ignore this," said Sister Karen as she pointed to the right place on the page for midday prayer. "Sister Katherine will be saying it."

Sister Katherine smiled at me. She was wearing her customary turtleneck and sweater, her face open and kind.

And so we began, reading the Psalms back and forth, with Sister Katherine adding the antiphon at the appropriate times.

A reading from the book of Isaiah, then another psalm. Soon, it was over, just a short fifteen or twenty minutes of prayer. Sister Katherine got up to leave for an appointment, but I stayed to chat with Sister Karen and Sister Mary Virginia for a while, who caught me up on how their sister Visitation Monastery, the one originally founded in St. Paul during the late 1800s by the city's Catholic elite, would be closing soon. The main ministry of the monastery was to run a Catholic school imbued in the traditions of Salesian spirituality and, while the school was still going strong, the number of nuns had dwindled down to just three.

Sister Mary Frances had been charged with helping the convent that had shaped her as a new novice die a good death. She traveled back and forth between North Minneapolis and its location in Mendota Heights, doing who knew what. How painful it must be, to see the convent close after over a hundred years of faithful service.

"Sister Mary Frances is helping them along," Sister Karen said. "But it will be a little while until the full monastery is suppressed."

"Suppressed," said Sister Mary Virginia, turning to me. "Isn't that an awful word?"

"Is that really what they call it? Suppressing a monastery?" I asked. Sister Karen and Mary Virginia nodded. "It sounds like someone is pushing it down, only to have it pop up elsewhere." I used a hand motion as I said this, pushing down with one hand and pulling up with the other.

"It's a hard thing," Sister Karen said, referring to the three remaining nuns in the closing monastery. "They really can't stay there anymore."

Later, in a conversation with Sister Brenda, she told me that I am following a "diminishment" narrative regarding the changes in religious orders. Many Catholic sisters, she told me, see the reduction of new sisters in their communities as "rightsizing" more than "downsizing." And some monastic orders are growing, particularly in the Global South.

But no matter how you frame it, to be part of the Western church in this century is to be in a community of decline. Many Christians in North America will watch their institutions die, their buildings close, their children walk away from organized religion.

I return to Amy's question: How can I love a dying thing? How can I hold onto faith as I watch so many of my peers walk away from the church?

There is much to mourn, and it will be painful, yet I can't help but watch the sisters with a glimmer of hope. Some communities are attracting younger sisters who will continue in vowed, religious life, but many will close their monasteries in the decades to come. The sisters who remain model a profound trust in the power of the Holy Spirit to take what has been lost and transform it into something new. To let go of control, to relinquish their communities to God, even as they keep casting sparks around in trust that something will catch fire.

The alternative is fear: holding things so closely they distort in my grasp. Instead, the Spirit calls me to let go, let go, let go. Relinquish Josh to God again and again. Richard Rohr writes, "It's like a secret spiral: each time you allow the surrender, each time you can trust the dying, you will experience a new quality of life within you."

To love a dying thing is to let it go, to let your love extend beyond religious conditions. To love a dying thing is to trust that, in the dying, Easter is still coming.

18

March 26

PALM SUNDAY

We were late for church. Josh pulled into a handicapped spot and dropped me and the kids off by the back entrance. I scrambled after them, an extra bag of kids' clothes draped over my arm, my blue travel mug of coffee tucked inside. "I have to pee!" my son told me as we climbed the steps. We walked down the narrow hallway to the nursery and ran into a cluster of kids by the doorway clutching palm branches. Amy, the smiling children's pastor, waved to us: "You're just in time!" and handed each child a palm. I pointed to the bathroom explaining "Bathroom emergency" and steered Rowan inside while Eliza joined the crowd of other kids.

After singing the Daniel Tiger potty-training song ("Flush and wash and be on your way!"), I opened the bathroom door to find the kids already gone. They must have begun the procession, I told my son, who looked stunned at the now empty hallway. We raced around the other side and entered the back of the sanctuary, watching the kids walking up and down the aisles waving branches as the gospel choir sang "Hosanna, Hail King Jesus" to a steady beat. Eliza was walking down the aisle toward us, so I waved and guided her little brother to join her in the procession. The adults were all smiles and cameras, and the beat of the drum thumped its way into my heart, crept upward toward my face, and crested into a grin. I can't help it—I love Palm Sunday. I love the servant King riding on a donkey, I love the pageantry and glorious drama of the Messiah, humble and powerful, making his way toward Jerusalem and his own death.

As a lifelong churchgoer, I've probably heard dozens of Palm Sunday sermons. At the Mennonite church, this Sunday was always one of great joys—it's the pinnacle of the peace-loving theology that Anabaptists center on. When Pastor Jeff began his sermon stating that Palm Sunday is primarily a story about expectations, I nodded to myself, confident that I knew where this was going. The Jews were expecting a victorious Messiah who would deliver them from their oppressor; they imagined a God who could redeem the righteous and pay back evil for evil, not a King who would die on a cross.

But this year at Calvary, the sermon took a turn I wasn't expecting. Pastor Jeff highlighted the prophecy from the book of Zechariah in the Old Testament about a king, lowly and riding on a donkey, who will come and destroy Israel's enemies. In the prophecy, God's people are told to "return to your fortress, you prisoners of hope" as they await God's redemptive and destructive work.

That "prisoners of hope" line, the preacher said, is what we need to hold on to. The Jewish people's expectation—that their lives, their nation, their future, would look a certain way—had not come to pass. In his own life, he said, there had been many times when what he had hoped for, what he'd asked God for, had not been realized. He had been deeply disappointed but remained a prisoner of hope. God gave us power, he said, power rooted in love and humility to live our lives like Jesus. But often it's not intuitive. It's not the way of this world, the way we expect.

I listened to these words as I sat alone in the pew, and I saw myself as very much a prisoner. It would be much easier to walk out of these doors forever, out of the struggle to bring my kids to church alone on Sundays, out of the nagging resentment toward my husband for not sitting beside me. Some days I want to do just that—to leave church, to let my faith slide, to change myself to fit where Josh is at, to spend Sunday mornings as a family going out for hikes or reading the newspaper at home. But something keeps dragging me back to church and Mass at the monastery, back to Palm Sunday after Palm Sunday.

The day before Palm Sunday had been one of the largest marches in US history, led by the teenagers who survived the Parkland, Florida, high school shooting. Pastor Jeff told us that anyone who wanted to wave their palm branches and carry a few signs about sensible gun laws could join us right after the service to march down Twenty-Sixth Street for a couple of blocks.

Yes! I thought to myself, excited. I wanted my kids to join in this example of a church community responding to injustice. So as the congregants started pushing out toward the street, I raced over to the nursery to grab my kids and join the procession. After zipping up coats and finding mittens, I held their hands—one on each side—and walked out the front doors of the church. Most of the marchers had already left. I pulled on my kids and started a slow jog, eager to catch up. It had only been a year since I started attending this church and, while I knew a few people, I didn't know many well. Most of the people ahead of me were in their nuclear family or friend groupings and walking at steady clip, and it wasn't long before we fell behind. I watched as dads hoisted their daughters onto their shoulders, as parents tag-teamed to carry kids.

"Mom," Rowan yelled, "I'm tired."

"Why are we doing this?" Eliza asked. "This isn't really doing anything, is it?" I considered her words as we walked along, unsuccessfully trying to keep up. A plastic bag floated on the wind by our feet. "We should be picking up trash," my daughter said. "Trash is what is hurting people, and the world God made, and the animals."

I explained a little of why we were marching as a church, but my voice trailed off. I picked up my son, who kept stopping to gather debris from the street (a stick, a hotel keycard, a straw) and considered the distance to the congregational marchers. They were a whole block ahead now, and we were just a party of three, holding scraggly palm branches and walking alone.

So much for this meaningful moment, I thought to myself, as Rowan brushed the palm branch against my face. I slowed my pace as the people marching ahead turned the corner, and when we reached the Dunn Brothers Coffee shop, I stopped.

"Hey," I told the kids. "Let's just go in here. I'll ask Dad to come get us."

I ordered a muffin and orange juice, then guided the kids to sit at the square tables by the window. I gathered the palm branches and put them on a nearby chair, then looked out the window at the gray March sky and tried not to cry. Who gets left behind in a Palm Sunday march? I wished that I had just asked some church members if we could walk with them. I wished someone had noticed we were falling behind.

"It's taken me years to get to know people at this church," my friend Julie told me later. "It takes dozens of tiny interactions, Sunday after Sunday, to break in. You have to keep showing your face, keep having conversations."

I picked at my muffin, then pushed it away. I texted Josh: "Will you come pick us up at the coffee shop?" I didn't want to walk back into the church today.

19

HOLY WEEK

*H*oly Week came the last week of March. Maybe it was the giant snowdrifts towering over the sidewalks, or the lingering hurt over being left behind in a hosanna march, but I didn't feel excitement for the long week of religious observance ahead. At our old Anglican church, Holy Week was a marathon of the faithful: we would parade on Palm Sunday, wash feet on Maundy Thursday, remember Jesus' crucifixion on Good Friday, then stage a three-hour Easter Vigil on Saturday night, culminating in bells and shouts of resurrection (my favorite part by far). But by the time Sunday morning service rolled around, we were exhausted. It was too much church for one week, and I could barely muster up a hallelujah.

This year, my Holy Week celebration included a return to therapy. On Wednesday after Mass at the monastery, I drove to the suburbs to meet with the marriage counselor that Josh and I had been seeing during the previous year. It had been a few months since we had been to counseling as a couple, but I scheduled this appointment for myself without realizing what week it was. I wanted to talk about my "spiritual singleness" revelation and the nuns.

I sat on the futon in the counselor's small office, taking sips of Tazo chai from a paper cup. After catching him up on the events of the last few months, I asked: "Is this whole quest a bit desperate?"

"No," my counselor said, taking off his glasses to rub the spot between his eyes. "It sounds to me like going through the formation program at the monastery has been good for you." I took another sip of black tea.

"What about spiritual singleness?" I asked him. "Did God speak to me in the woods or am I losing my mind?"

He laughed. "I can't verify if God spoke to you. But I do think spiritual singleness can be a useful term. It's a healthy form of self-differentiation in your marriage."

Self-differentiation. That sounded important, so I wrote it down in my journal, which I had brought to the appointment, and circled it. Twice.

Later at home, when I googled the term, I read articles about people who have a strong sense of self: their priorities, their opinions, their boundaries firm and distinct from their loved ones. On a family therapy website, self-differentiation was described as "being able to have different opinions and values than your family members, but being able to stay emotionally connected to them."

I wondered if that was part of my problem in the years since Josh left Christianity, when I struggled to follow Jesus and live out my faith's upside-down principles without him. How could we stay emotionally connected while believing in and valuing different things?

MAUNDY THURSDAY

There was no evening foot washing service at Calvary for Maundy Thursday, so I read the familiar stories about the Last Supper in *Give Us This Day* at home instead. In the gospel story of the upper room, Peter pleads with Jesus to wash "not just my feet but my hands and head as well!" Judas, the disciple who would go on to betray Jesus for thirty pieces of silver, also had his feet washed and dried by Jesus.

"What if Judas had . . . been able to forgive Jesus for not being the kind of savior he thought he should be?" wrote Rachelle Linner in the daily reflection from *Give Us This Day*. "Can we learn from what he couldn't do and forgive others for not being what we want them to be?"

I set down the prayer book on the couch beside me and closed my eyes. Could I forgive Josh for not being a Christian? And could Josh forgive me for not changing with him?

GOOD FRIDAY

"Hey, are you going to a service?" Josh asked. He was lying on the living room carpet, using a foam roller to loosen his quads after a long run. I had just gotten out of the shower and had my towel wrapped around me.

"Calvary doesn't have one until seven, and that's too late," I said. "It's already after three. I think the one at Ascension Catholic Church is starting now."

"Go! You should go," he said.

"Really?" I said, looking down at my towel, at my bare toes.

"Yes," he said, throwing a balled-up sock at me from the floor. "The church is what, five minutes away? You have time. You should go."

I dried my hair, threw on some clothes, and hopped in the car. Josh was right. It was just five minutes away.

I was still late, but not by much. I entered the back of the sanctuary and picked up a bulletin from a side table. The service was underway, and I scanned the program to try and find my place. The priest was leading the congregation through something called "The Solemn Intercessions." I picked up the prayer book, leafed through it for a moment, then joined the congregation in standing and speaking aloud the written prayers.

But I blinked hard when I read the title of Solemn Intercession VII: *For those who do not believe in God.* There, in print, in a Catholic prayer book no less, was a prayer for Josh.

I joined the rumble of the congregation as we spoke the words, together: "Let us pray also for those who do not acknowledge God, that, following what is right in sincerity of heart, they may find the way to God himself."

Following what is right in sincerity of heart, they may find the way to God.

I looked around the church at the stations of the cross, where vivid sculptures of Jesus' crucifixion story circled the sanctuary. This solemn intercession, like Jesus' prayer in the Garden of Gethsemane, was a prayer of trust and relinquishment. I could pray that Josh search his heart for what is right, and that by doing so he might find his way to God. It was a gentle prayer and one I wasn't praying alone. A whole congregation—the whole holy Catholic Church in Good Friday services around the world—was praying it with me.

Next, came a procession of the cross down the center aisle of the church. Incense swayed from side to side. The liturgy repeated the phrase: "Behold the wood of the Cross, on which hung the salvation of the world." Men carried a heavy cross through the church, then laid it at the front of the sanctuary.

People began to walk forward to show their signs of reverence—kneeling, kissing the cross. I came forward too, giving the cross a quick peck on the cheek as it were, wondering if my lips were touching the same grains of wood as the people before me. The wood felt soft on my lips.

At home, when I cracked open my book on Salesian spirituality, I read a quote from Saint Francis de Sales: "To take up our cross and follow Jesus Christ means nothing other than receiving and accepting all the troubles, contradictions, afflictions and mortifications that come our way in life."

Following Jesus means accepting all the troubles and contradictions? It's a hard teaching, especially in a solution-oriented culture. But it was easier to kiss the face of the cross after asking God to bless the journey of those who don't believe in God.

HOLY SATURDAY

It was just another Saturday in late winter. The kids played dress up and bickered over who got to use the purple marker. Josh met up with friends to go for a long run, so I made breakfast for the kids on my own. When I felt bored, I looked at my phone or took pictures of the kids in their pajamas and texted them to our relatives far away. After lunch we got our taxes done and found out we owed over one thousand dollars to the state government. As the kids watched episodes of *Ninjago* on the iPad, I put on my boots and walked through the snow in the backyard just to breathe the cold air, to feel it circulate in my lungs. I wondered if the tulip bulbs had sprouted under the snow banks.

EASTER SUNDAY

Easter Sunday fell on April Fools' Day. On social media I saw a meme of Jesus re-appearing from the dead with a text bubble from his lips: "Gotcha!"

We hadn't talked about it, but I assumed Josh was coming to church with me and the kids on Easter morning. But it turned out we were not on the same page. I got huffy and slammed a door. He was impatient and barked at the kids to hurry up and put on their shoes already. The kids felt our bad mood; Rowan threw his shoe across the room instead of putting it on, and Eliza walked over to touch my side, looking for some kind of reassurance.

We fought more on the drive to church. He was going too fast, weaving around slower drivers, and I told him he was going to give me a heart attack.

"You don't have to come," I told him when we pulled through the alley behind the church, even though we both knew it wasn't true.

"I'm coming," he said.

I looked at the towering church spire from the car window. It was built in 1884, and it had been sitting on this corner for over a century. A young family walked in the back door, the parents holding hands.

"I don't even like this church," I said, turning away, remembering the loneliness of Palm Sunday.

"What?" Eliza asked. "Mama, what did you say?"

"I didn't mean that, I'm sorry," I said immediately, my cheeks hot.

There were no parking spots, so Josh pulled through the alley to go around the block. He parallel parked and we got out of the car and walked two blocks, our boots trailing through slush. Inside, there was the sound of gospel music. I didn't recognize the people we passed in the hallway. We first dropped the kids in the nursery, then entered the sanctuary together. It was the first time since Christmas Eve that Josh attended an entire service with me. I folded my arms as we walked side-by-side.

In the sermon, Pastor Jeff started by sharing an Easter in his past when he hadn't understood the hope of this holiday. He said, "Yeah, so what, Jesus was raised from the dead, but that doesn't change the reality out in the real world." It was like the meme of Jesus playing a divine prank on April Fools' and yelling "Gotcha!" after jumping from behind the tombstone.

He described his journey from that place of cynicism to one of wonder. He played a short video, the film projected on a white wall to the left of the pulpit. It was about the moon, the way it can evoke the feeling of mystery. It's a wonder that all humans can share in. It was this shift into awe that saved his faith, he said.

It was a new understanding that the Scriptures are like poetry, that they give us a story we can find ourselves in, that they point to something where we can find hope.

After the sermon was over, the associate pastor got up and introduced Communion. "This table," she said, stretching her arms wide, "is a table for all of us. It's not a table that belongs to religion, it's not a table that belongs to the church. This table belongs to the Lord. All of you are welcome here."

We were seated near the front of the church, and I moved to stand up and join the line of people filing forward to tear off a piece of bread and dip it in the chalice. Josh moved behind me. He was following me to the altar.

"Are you sure?" I whispered to him, incredulous.

"She said everyone is welcome, didn't she?" he said.

I smiled. Maybe I did like this church.

When Josh first stopped coming to church with me, I felt it most strongly when I took Communion alone. Communion is a sign of the unity of the church and, at our wedding, Josh and I had served the sacrament together to our family and friends. But since he deconverted, Josh no longer ate the bread nor drank from the common cup; he was outside the body of Christ. The old metaphors of two becoming one flesh in marriage felt at stake. Were we still "one" in our union? How did we understand our commitment, our community now?

Most Christian teaching is clear that only professed believers should take Communion, and plenty of churches deny the sacrament to those outside their denomination. I am sure I have unknowingly broken rules myself as a baptized Presbyterian by receiving Communion in a variety of churches over the years. The underlying theology is important; my reforming ancestors— Lutherans, Mennonites, and the like—endured persecution for different understandings of the sacraments. But even if I understand this intellectually, I could weep in gratitude for the associate pastor's open invitation. "Take, eat," she had said. "This is Christ's body, broken for you."

Jesus ate regularly with outsiders. When he caught flack for doing so, he replied: "It is not the healthy who need a doctor, but the sick. I have not come to call the righteous, but sinners."

Later I asked Josh about taking Communion on Easter. He repeated that he had felt welcomed to join this spiritual practice because of the associate pastor's words. He didn't say it, but I wondered if he also took Communion for me—to support me by joining in this mystical ritual, to show me I am not alone.

I don't understand it. But I feel a prickling of hope—not for Josh's conversion back to faith, exactly, but that he, too, might be hungry for a taste of God's goodness.

20

SPIRITUAL WEATHER REPORT

*T*wo days after Easter, new snow fell overnight. Outside my window I saw a parent and child walking to the bus stop, their boots trudging through fresh snow, their faces bent downward. Snow in April isn't unusual in Minnesota, though this year the steady cold temperatures were chillier than average. Last spring, the winter had slipped away so gradually that I hardly noticed it. It was just the beginning of the Easter season, but winter was not letting go.

It started as a cold rain. I was walking in my neighborhood and asking God for strength to relinquish Josh and his faith journey all over again. I prayed for our marriage, for greater faith in God's goodness, for trust that God was even listening as I plodded along. Maybe God would speak back, but all I could hear were the sounds of my feet on pavement, my feet crackling on thin sheets of ice.

When I looked up, the world had suddenly gone white. Earlier, the weather report had said "snow-rain mix." The temperature must have just dipped from 33 to 32 degrees, the necessary condition for rain to become snow.

The sky was now thick with white clumping flakes, like in the movies when kids have pillow fights at slumber parties and the air fills with floating feathers. An instant transformation—gray rain into a world of white. When I got home, I stood inside by the big picture window and watched it coming down in earnest: flakes darting and swirling, then disappearing as they hit the warm ground. When it snows in April, you know it won't stick around for long.

All it took for that change, from liquid to solid, was the air temperature—an invisible change suddenly made visible.

When does doubt turn to unbelief? What is the temperature at which any certainty melts away? Can I still be a Christian if my faith is a wintry mix, one that fluctuates between rain and sleet and snow?

I once believed that a steady, certain faith in God and the Nicene Creed and the Bible was an absolute requirement for being a Christian. But in my own faith journey, the temperature keeps fluctuating and I can't seem to control the weather. I just keep walking and talking to God, keep taking the next set of steps, keep dressing for whatever the weather.

Saint Francis de Sales, patron saint of writers that he is, uses the metaphor of spiritual weather as well. Weather fluctuations are to be expected and sometimes, Francis writes, we can't always identify a cause for them. Some days we are full of joy but, he warns, "the fine, pleasant weather will not always last." Often, it's followed by a state that feels like "barren, sterile desert where there is no path or road to God." In this case, Francis suggests that you "not be too eager to be released from this state of dryness but rather wait calmly until God himself relieves it. . . . At all costs, let us never lose courage in time of aridity but wait patiently."

I suspect that waiting for God, even with all my uncertainties, looks like showing up in what Saint Francis calls "the sauce of life"—the immutable, unchanging realities of my day to day. I am a mother and a wife and a writer. I have a job and a family and a mortgage. I am choosing to stay married to someone who doesn't believe in God, and he is choosing to stay married to me.

What separates my faith from Josh's, even as my own belief fluctuates depending on the day? Why do I keep walking (albeit badly) in the rituals and rhythms of Christian practice: the Sunday services, praying the Psalms with the nuns, taking Communion at church?

The evangelical tradition in which our faith was formed always hammered down the importance of right belief. All it took to be a Christian was believing that Jesus was the Son of God, that he died on the cross for our sins, and that we must accept him into our hearts to achieve eternal life. Having all the right answers seemed so simple.

Is it any surprise that many former evangelicals, who took this emphasis of right belief so seriously, eventually walk away when their doubts begin to feel overwhelming? Look, they might say. The temperature changed. It's not snowing anymore. It's rain. Might as well call it what it is.

I suspect that most people don't experience their faith as fixed, that conversion and deconversion binaries are more fluid than we sometimes admit. Being part of any religion is less about how we feel or what we believe at any given instant, which changes moment by moment, and more about our commitment to wrestle with our faith. But what made me hold onto God when Josh let go? Was it grace? Free will? Predestination? Was I called and Josh not called? Was his baptism erased?

Recently Josh told me that leaving Christianity is one of the things he feels most proud of in his life. He stopped pretending he still believed in God. He stopped pretending he still saw snow.

"It's hard to hear you talk about being proud of something that has hurt me," I told him while we stood in the kitchen.

"You know I didn't mean it like that," he said. "It's just that I finally broke free of something that wasn't good for me anymore."

I nodded. I sighed. "I know. I know." When Josh described to me what his faith had been like when he was a Christian, he spoke about fear—fear of never pleasing God, fear of never being good enough. It made it hard for him to experience God's love. I told him I wasn't sure if I believed in the God he described, either.

But I can't stop thinking about Josh taking Communion. It was the first time we have shared that practice in over four years. I wrote an email to Pastor Jeff yesterday, thanking him for his Easter sermon and remarking that the extended winter weather felt like Holy Saturday all over again. There are zero chances of spring not coming, at least eventually, and yet for how long will we wait? This April is not meeting my expectations for green grass, new life, and fresh growth.

It's not unlike the experience after a religious high—a week at Bible camp, an experience of God at the top of a mountain—and the inevitable, subsequent letdown. Okay, Christ has risen from the dead. So what? Okay, Easter is over—but nothing is different. So Josh took Communion—but he still doesn't believe in God. Winter is still holding on, and I see no visible signs that anything has changed.

Holy Saturday isn't just a day we remember once a year but the name of a real emotional state for those of us who are waiting for the kingdom of God, for any sign that God cares and is present and wants to fulfill all those covenantal promises.

Easter Sunday came and went, but the real work is loving the world as it actually is. As Saint Francis writes, we are not to "waste our energy hankering after a different sort of life but get on with our own."

21

May 3

ELISABETH LESEUR

*I*n all my reading on the saints, I haven't found many examples of relatable married women. Most of the female saints in *Give Us This Day* are either martyrs, or virgin-martyrs, or intrepid foundresses of monastic communities. Saint Jane de Chantal was once married, sure, but her life only became saint material after her husband was shot in a hunting accident. Not exactly helpful advice for those of us with husbands who are very much alive.

But then I met a new mystical sister: Elisabeth Leseur. Not only was she married to an atheist, but, like me, she teetered on the edge of Christian belief herself at one time in her life.

Born in 1866, Elisabeth was from a Catholic family and lived during a time of anticlericalism and rapid secularization in her native France. As biographer Wendy Wright put it, Elisabeth "found herself married to an unbeliever in an age of unbelief."

Married to an unbeliever in an age of unbelief. Well, that sure sounds familiar.

Like me, Elisabeth knew the social tension of living out her faith when religious practice was on the decline. She was privileged and well connected, her circles decidedly sophisticated and secular. Elisabeth's environment had a big effect on her, and she wasn't all that serious about her faith in the early years of her marriage. Her husband, Felix, was strident in his antireligious convictions and tried to discourage Elisabeth from Catholic practice. He even gave her books on liberal Protestantism, which he hoped would act as "a stage on the way to radical agnosticism."

Elisabeth read the antireligious books Felix gave her and was unimpressed. She disagreed with the arguments on an intellectual basis, which she found flimsy, and turned to the Gospels to read for herself what Jesus had to say. Elisabeth "felt herself approach the abyss" of deconversion but ultimately "sprang backward."

Here is where her story gets especially interesting: Elisabeth experienced a mystical return to faith, but she also made a personal, ascetic commitment to "an almost absolute silence" about her interior life. She began to practice her faith privately and did not speak to Felix about her devotion. It was only after her death that Felix learned of how deep and fervent her faith life had been.

What kind of marriage is this? I thought while reading Elisabeth's spiritual writings. *Who keeps something as big as her faith secret from her husband?*

But as strange (and impractical) as living a secret faith while being married might seem, I think Elisabeth might have something to teach me.

When I blather on to Josh about the sermon he missed, neither of us ends up feeling very happy. To me the conversations—or personal monologues—only reinforce our spiritual division; for his part, Josh wonders if I am subtly trying to convert him. (I'm not!) Elisabeth believed that "arguments or discussion was futile and would never be persuasive with the kinds of unbelievers she knew" and instead hoped God's divine presence would shine through her to those around her. In turn, keeping my faith private might help me to focus less on Josh's spirituality and more on my own.

It makes sense that Elisabeth was a devotee of Saint Francis de Sales, who emphasized holiness in all walks of life. "Be who you are and be that well" is a famous maxim attributed to De Sales, and Elisabeth practiced radical acceptance of her marriage to an atheist.

If my marriage therapist had been the one to tell Elisabeth about "self-differentiation," she would have stared, crossed her waifish arms across her chest, and uttered a "duh" in a French accent. Elisabeth believed that "in order to surrender herself entirely to God and God's will for her, she had a responsibility to cultivate and develop her fullest potential." In her years of secret practice, Elisabeth developed a personal rule of life—without waiting around for her husband—that involved study and prayer. In particular, she adopted the principles of flexibility and charity, making sure that her devotion wasn't disruptive to those around her.

Even though Elisabeth wasn't exactly waiting around for Felix to join her for Mass, she did pray fervently for his conversion all the time. It's a good thing my first encounter with Elisabeth was in a book on lay sanctity and not her posthumously published diary, otherwise I probably would have written her off just for its subtitle: *The Woman Whose Goodness Changed Her Husband from Atheist to Priest*. This part of Elisabeth's story chafes the most at my modern sensibilities. Why is her goodness responsible for his conversion? She literally made a pact with God that, in exchange for her sufferings, God would convert her husband after her death and turn him into a priest. Which, of course, happened. She wouldn't be a candidate for sainthood if it hadn't.

I suppose this is why her cause for beatification was opened in 1990—because her story is miraculous. An atheist becomes a priest, and all because of his now-dead wife's prayers! It's not an ordinary story of a women like me who struggles with faith, who struggles to pray for her husband. Because, what's saintly about that?

If Elisabeth were here in the room with me, I imagine that she would reach across and grip my shoulders, straightening my rounded back, and force me to make eye contact.

"I, too, stared into the abyss of unbelief," I imagine she would say to me. "But God turned me back into his arms. Don't despair. Devote yourself to Christ, and trust that God will act."

22

ON VOWS

*M*ost of the Visitation Sisters I know joined the convent when they were young: nineteen, twenty, twenty-five. At the same age when their peers were getting married and starting families, these women were taking lifelong vows to celibacy, to live in community, to submit their own wills and desires to a rule of life devised by Saint Francis and Saint Jane over four hundred years ago.

But one morning in early May, Sister Karen invited me to come to something unusual: a first profession of vows for a woman in her fifties. Sister Brenda was formally entering the community. She had an unusual story: after living for decades as a Baptist missionary in Asia, Brenda had been confirmed in the Catholic Church just five years before, when she came to live and pray with the sisters at Visitation Monastery. She was an anomaly, an outlier, and a full twenty years younger than the next older sister in the community.

The first vows service was held at Ascension Catholic Church, where I had kissed the cross on Good Friday and where the sisters went to church each Sunday. I walked over from my house, making my way down Fremont to Broadway, passing empty lots and the newly opened gas station on the corner. The grass was a luminous green. A group of kids biked back and forth on the sidewalk while music blared from an open window. Trees were just starting to leaf out, their branches bobbing with mini leaves. The snow had finally melted and new life was emerging everywhere.

After walking past Broadway's bus stops and storefronts and honking traffic, I turned right on Bryant Avenue. Already I could see the red brick and sandstone of the church, the towering white spire looming over the intersection a few blocks away. When it was founded in 1890, Ascension Catholic Church was home to Irish and German immigrants who lived in the surrounding Old Highland neighborhood. Now the Gothic-style church holds Masses in both English and Spanish, serving more recent immigrants to this area.

What would a first vows ceremony be like? I wondered. *And what had led Brenda from a life as a Baptist missionary to a life as a Catholic nun?*

I marched my way up the concrete stairs of the church, opened the heavy wooden doors, and walked into the sanctuary, which was about half full. Someone played a piano prelude in the background amid rumbles of chatter. Middle-aged people in church clothes—pastels and suit jackets, skirts and nylons—greeted one another, they hugged and shook hands. I looked down at my jeans, trying to smooth the wrinkles in my blouse before sliding into a pew behind two older women I recognized from Wednesday Mass at the monastery. The front of the church was decorated with potted flowers, all lavenders and pinks and cheerful mums. On a small table covered with a white cloth sat cut pink flowers in a glass vase, a white pillar candle, and a stand holding a heavy-looking, brown book.

Sister Mary Frances, dressed in a smart white pantsuit, welcomed the crowd. Processional music began, and a stream of people walked down the center aisle led by a woman carrying a tall, bronze crucifix. People carried candles, and one man in a white alb swung a bronze ball of incense back and forth, leaving a smoky perfume in the air.

Brenda appeared next, wearing a crimson brocade jacket and a corsage of roses and baby's breath. She walked down the aisle with her mother. Next, her two biological sisters walked down the center aisle, followed by the Visitation nuns, two by two: Suzanne and Katherine, Mary Virginia and Karen. Finally, Mary Francis wheeled in Mary Margaret, who looked fragile and thin framed in the chair. It was the first time I had laid eyes on this founding sister of the monastery, who I often heard referred to as the "resident mystic." She had just celebrated her ninetieth birthday and was mostly confined to her upstairs bedroom in the Girard House following a debilitating stroke. The sisters hired a skilled caregiver to come in the mornings, and they took turns sitting with her, acting, they said, as "Mary Margaret's afternoon angel."

The Visitation Sisters filed into the front pew, like seven beads on a string. I watched Brenda's mother and sisters settle into a row behind them, and I wondered what her Protestant family thought of all this Catholic business, of the porcelain stations of the cross that ringed the sanctuary, of the statue of Mary in the alcove, of the dramatic white spires behind the altar, of the life-sized, bloody Jesus hanging on a wooden cross off to the side.

Had her mother instead imagined a wedding for her child, processing down the aisle someday in a humble Baptist church with no graven images of God, no special veneration of Mary or suspicious medieval saints, as a mother of the bride? Had she prayed for her Brenda's spouse since she was a little girl, just as Josh's mother once told me she had done for him?

The parallels to a wedding were inescapable: the corsage, the procession down the aisle, the vows. Presiding over the Mass was Father Dale, who remarked that there had not been a vow ceremony for a religious vocation at Ascension Church in decades.

Brenda had been a novice for two years prior, spending her novitiate studying the Visitation vows and living as a fully integrated member of the monastic community. Her experience is a very different one than many of the other Catholic sisters in the community, most of whom were novices before Vatican II when they wore special habits and didn't see their family members for months upon entering the enclosure. In those days, first vows were even more like a wedding—some women wore wedding dresses as they became the brides of Christ.

Some nuns really get into the nuptial metaphors—their marriages to Jesus, their identity as Christ's brides. But when I asked Sister Katherine later if she feels married to Jesus, she scoffed. Some people, she said, have this overly romantic idea when they make their monastic vows. (I later read in a book about the Visitation Sisters' vocation stories that Sister Mary Frances, who once had a young man very interested in her romantically, heard

God say to her: "I want you for myself." This voice confirmed for her that she should join the convent instead.)

There is no theology in my tradition that encourages women to eschew marriage. Yet in one of Paul's letters, he recommends Christ followers *not* to marry. Even Jesus says so in Luke's gospel. When did that clear biblical admonition fall out of favor with evangelicals? Is there something very Protestant about rejecting celibacy as an honored way to serve God?

When I interviewed Brenda a few months later, she spoke to me about how hard it was to be a single woman in the Baptist church. "They didn't know what to do with me," she laughed, then described the tediously titled "Spares and Pairs" social groups in Texas churches where single women like her were essentially compared to extra parts. Even in the missionary community, it was hard to be single when most others were married with children. It's no wonder that the monastery, with its rhythms of daily prayer, would be compelling in comparison.

Joining a monastic order is more than heeding the call to singleness, she told me. It's about making vows to God and committing to live them out in community.

A few years back, Josh and I attended a different kind of vows ceremony—a wedding. We borrowed a minivan and drove to a family wedding in North Carolina, placating our antsy children with audiobooks and dry Cheerios during the long drive from my in-laws' home. It had been threatening rain and stormy weather from the high winds at the coast that caused flooding in

Louisiana. The sky was mottled with dark clouds. I leaned across the seat to where my husband was driving, touching his arm. "Look at the sky! Those clouds are brooding."

"You've always loved a moody sky," he said, grinning. He was right. "Let's just hope it doesn't rain."

The wedding was at one of those farms-turned-event venues complete with a grain silo, distressed wooden fences, and a red vintage tractor. Everything was Pinterest worthy, from to the hand-lettered bulletins to the engagement photos framed in old windowpanes. Four-year-old Eliza snatched several of the complimentary sunglasses in delight, skipping down the mowed path to the wedding site. We sat on benches toward the back as we waited for the wedding to start, letting then-toddler Rowan wander to the edges where tall grass stood. Menacing clouds loomed overhead, but the rain held off.

One thing I can appreciate about a Baptist wedding is that ceremonies are generally short, cutting down the number of times we had to scary-whisper "be quiet" to our kids. The preacher didn't give a sermon but rather facilitated something called the unity cross. The bride and groom each held parts of a cross: he, a metal cross outline and she, a curlicue wrought-iron piece that fit inside his. The preacher explained that the groom's piece of the cross represents the protection, strength, and leadership he provides his bride, while the bride's piece of the cross represents the beauty and many capabilities of the woman that fit inside her husband's protection.

When they fit the pieces together to complete the cross, I fidgeted with my program and glanced over at Eliza, who was

BLESSED ARE THE NONES

too busy poking her cousin and fiddling with her new sunglasses to pay attention. The preacher continued by placing three pegs in the completed cross, representing the Father, the Son, and the Holy Spirit, to hold the sculpture—and marriage—together.

"Marriage is only possible through God," the preacher said. "And God is the only foundation that can support a lasting commitment."

That statement, plus the male headship theology in the unity cross, made me want to run for the hills. I leaned over to Josh again and gave his hand a desperate squeeze. He squeezed back.

The couple turned to look at each other and made their vows. Benedictine sister and feminist Joan Chittister once wrote that vows, whether in marriage or in monasticism, are intended to be a "public witness to Gospel values." I softened as the couple spoke their solemn promises, which they had written themselves. They were beautiful. Vows are something, Chittister writes, to "take heart from, take hope from."

After the ceremony, we walked over to the barn for the reception—our children now going rogue and plowing through tall prairie grasses, looking for grasshoppers to catch—and I briefly wondered if we were doing it all wrong. We also got married outdoors at a farm-turned-wedding venue; we also pledged to make God the foundation of our marriage covenant. What if the preacher was right, that God is the only foundation that can support a lasting commitment? Did the vows Josh and I had made still reflect Gospel values? Would they last?

Our wedding ceremony was not short. No less than three clergy officiated: Josh's Baptist pastor grandfather (gave the welcoming prayer), my Presbyterian pastor mother (preached the homily and officiated our vows), and our Episcopalian priest at the time (celebrated Communion). Given the trinity of presiding pastors, who represented a mishmash of Christian traditions, we simplified by using a-straight-out-of-the-book liturgy.

You may have heard it before. It begins "Dearly beloved, we are gathered here today . . ." The vows from a "Celebration and Blessing of a Marriage" in the *Book of Common Prayer* are simple, traditional, and direct. We promised to have and to hold, in sickness and in health, till death us do part. As egalitarians, we committed to mutual submission in our union.

After we made our vows, the pastor prayed a blessing over us, asking for God's assistance and grace "that with true fidelity and steadfast love they may honor and keep the promises and vows they make." True fidelity. Steadfast love. Honoring and keeping promises and vows. In the photos from our ceremony, you can see the pillar-like clouds over our heads that some guests told us were a sign of the Holy Spirit.

Back in North Carolina, as we inched through the buffet line, greedily heaping our plates with pulled pork, coleslaw, and cornbread with honey butter, my brother and sisters-in-law chatted excitedly about the fact that this wedding—unlike any of the other family weddings they'd attended—had a dance floor and DJ. The small, independent Baptist church where Josh's grandfather ministered for decades didn't allow dancing in its fellowship hall.

After we ate too much barbecue and drank our sugary sweet teas, our table of "young marrieds" jumped up to watch the first dance between the new husband and wife. They slow danced to some top-40 love song that I was too out-of-touch to recognize, and Eliza stood on the sidelines, her hands clasped together, a shy smile on her face as she watched them sway and kiss.

Other married couples were then invited to join in the dancing. At one point the DJ announced, "Will all the couples who have been married for one year or less please exit the dance floor." After a few moments he continued, dismissing couples who had been married two, five, ten years, and so on. Finally, only my husband's grandparents were left. The DJ kept counting until he reached sixty years.

"Wow, folks, sixty years," the DJ said, stepping out on the dance floor and approaching the couple with his microphone.

"Do you have any marital wisdom that you can share with this new couple?" he asked, pointing the microphone in Josh's grandfather's face.

He looked around, then said, "The only advice I have is adjust, adjust, adjust!" Everyone laughed.

✥❧

When Josh first deconverted, a friend asked me if I thought this was grounds for dissolving the marriage. "Isn't this a violation of the vows?" she asked me. The traditional Episcopal liturgy, which we used in our wedding, was centered on God through Jesus Christ our Lord. If Josh was no longer a Christian, did that nullify our marriage? Her question caught me off-guard.

Not all marriages can (or should) survive a faith-shift; sometimes people can't make their love "free of religious conditions," as my friend Caroline had said. Sometimes people change in unhealthy or destructive or abusive ways, and the vows need to be broken.

Still, I want to believe that our vows are holy despite the ways we have changed. That marriage is not a dated institution but a means for God to refine us into better versions of our selves. That *adjust, adjust, adjust* is like a polishing rag, not a pounding cleaver. Some days I'm not so sure. I don't want to resent Josh for not being a Christian. In our most honest moments, Josh has told me that he wishes I had lost my faith too.

I will never know what the experience of living a lifelong monastic calling is like, of entering a convent at age nineteen or even fifty, but I do know something about honoring vows. I wore a white dress and held Josh's hands and we made promises to each other at age twenty-five that we had no idea how to keep. In her book *Acedia and Me*, Kathleen Norris wrote: "The very nature of marriage means saying yes before you know what it will cost. Though you may say the 'I do' of the wedding ritual in all sincerity, it is the testing of that vow over time that makes you married."

There is no doubt that vows are what hold marriages and monastic communities together; they make stability possible. But vows can be costly; our partners and institutions change, we change, and sixty years is a long time to live with someone you fell in love with at age eighteen.

Maybe how we understand those vows needs to change as well.

Benedictine Sister Joan Chittister has written extensively about the vows of religious life, criticizing their outdated framework. She wrote: "What the world needs now, respects now, demands now, understands now is not poverty, chastity and obedience. It is generous justice, reckless love and limitless listening." I love the way Chittister reimagines the commitments she and her fellow sisters have made, expanding their definitions to make room for a new era.

Later when I ask Sister Brenda about her vow ceremony, she tells me that many religious women rearticulate their vows when they celebrate twenty-five, fifty, or sixty years. "While each congregation has a vow formula that they recite at first vows, we often rewrite them for ourselves and our own understanding," she said.

Maybe Josh and I will rewrite our vows using new language that reflects who we are now, like my friend Caroline and her husband, Jake, did. But even if we do, we don't need a ceremony to renew our vows. We renew them each time we give each other permission to change or when we reject fear. We renew them each time we choose to connect beyond our spiritual identities, when we have empathy for each other's struggles.

Regardless of what words we use to articulate our vows, it's our stability, our fidelity, that "makes growth possible by forcing us to choose and choose again." Our vows are only as strong as the way we live them, day after day.

23

May 31

FEAST OF THE VISITATION

*O*f all the stories about women saints I've encountered so far this year, it's the relationship between Mary and Elizabeth that has most surprised me.

The Visitation is a Bible story about two pregnant women prophesying over each other: Mary is newly pregnant, and her cousin Elizabeth is six months along. Mary comes to visit, and the two women share a remarkable moment. John the Baptist, who is gestating in Elizabeth's womb, leaps inside her, and Elizabeth is filled with the Holy Spirit. She proclaims in a loud voice that Mary is blessed among women and that the child she carries is also blessed. "Blessed is she who has believed that the Lord would fulfill his promises to her!" Mary is astonished at her older relative's words and in response sings one of the most famous and subversive songs in the Bible: the Magnificat.

Elizabeth's prophecy makes Mary the first saint, forever setting Mary apart as special. That part makes sense to me.

Women tell women the truth of the matter; they recognize the stories of God written all over each other's lives.

The monastery down the street is named after this Bible story, but the first time I heard its name, I wasn't sure whether the Visitation referred to the angel of the Lord visiting Mary (nope, that's the Annunciation) or something else entirely. I was confused because I didn't grow up hearing the story of the Visitation often—in part, I think, because the Protestant churches I've attended tend to ignore Mary. In the Catholic Church, the Visitation is more well known. It's considered the second joyful mystery of the rosary, which Catholics are taught to meditate on when praying.

The Visitation story is pictured all over the monastery. Over the fireplace at the Fremont house, a painting by Brother Mickey McGrath depicts Mary and Elizabeth as African queens in kente cloth embracing one another. A statue of two native women holding one another is fused into a single piece of stone, the dress of Elizabeth swirling and enfolding that of Mary. This special relationship is evident in the spirit, or charism, of the Visitation Sisters. It's a mutuality, an honoring of one another, a hospitality and welcome of a sister's presence. It is also a fulfillment of a prophecy—where one woman confirms the special calling in another's life. It's a recognition of the holy, the literal indwelling of God, and the prophetic response in Mary's song— that God comes to uplift the needy and to scatter the proud.

Notice there are no males in this story (besides those in utero). Mary and Elizabeth don't need their husbands' "spiritual headship" to recognize the inner workings of the Spirit or to preach God's truth in new and miraculous ways. Zechariah, Elizabeth's husband, has been struck mute because he didn't believe the angel, and at this point Joseph doesn't even know his fiancée is pregnant. The miracles of God, like in the Resurrection story, are first revealed to the women.

A man I met at the monastery said that the hospitality of the Visitation Monastery allows the soul to show itself, that the feeling of welcome brings out our truest selves. It's an unveiling—it reveals the state of our hearts; it is a means for God to show up in our lives. It is the condition needed for prophecy, for God's love to be embodied, for us to understand the truth about who we are and how God is present. These soul friends help us know God. The man also mentioned the words of John O'Donohue, who writes about *anam cara*, or spiritual friends. A soul without a spiritual companion is like a body without a head. We need community. We need companions on our spiritual journey.

Like Mary, I was nine months pregnant during Advent. Twice. The first time, Josh was a Christian, and the second time he wasn't. I can't remember if we prayed together for our first child when we were waiting for her birth, though it's likely we did. Between those births was another pregnancy, one that lasted only six weeks. I had slid down the stairs while holding our two-year-old, keeping her upright and unharmed but slamming my side down on the cheap university-housing carpet, hard. I bled heavily for days, the new life in my body leaking out. When had the baby died?

The miscarriage happened in November, just a few weeks before Advent began, just a month before I overheard the conversation in which Josh told his father he was not a Christian anymore. I wondered what I had done wrong—if it had been the fall on the stairs, if I had missed too many prenatal vitamins, if I hadn't been vigilant enough to keep that fluttering heart from stopping.

Two Advents, two healthy babies born in December. And one miscarriage in between, one death. Two Advents, three years apart, and one deconversion in between. A fall down the stairs. Faith that leaked away.

The nurse at the clinic told me that early miscarriages like mine are very common, that oftentimes there is something wrong with the embryo early on that makes it unviable.

I wonder whether Elizabeth had miscarriages. The Bible tells us that she was barren, but it never says whether she ever lost an early pregnancy. When she got pregnant with John the Baptist, did she harbor fear in her heart that maybe he, too, would die? Did she mistrust her own body's capacity to bear and sustain new life to full term, to be more than a vessel of death?

I never expected to relate to Mary and Elizabeth, but like them, female friendships have always been catalysts for transformation in my spiritual life. My mother prayed with me at night when I was a child. Church ladies drove vans to youth group lock-ins and brought homemade brownies to confirmation class. Female college students led Bible studies at summer camp and Young Life groups in high school.

When I was pregnant with my firstborn, two other friends were also pregnant and due around the same time. We took a photo together at my baby shower, our bodies turned to show our profiles, an adorable lineup of baby bumps. We commiserated over morning sickness stories; we compared notes about birth centers and midwives. We organized meal trains for each other, making sure family and friends didn't all bring lasagna. Once the babies were born and the winter faded into a mild spring, we met at Lake of the Isles and carried our newborns on the walking path, their bodies strapped tightly to our chests in Ergo carriers.

Those early years of babies and Josh's deconversion were hard. Interrupted sleep, mastitis, leaky breastmilk. Bundling up a toddler and a screaming baby, shuffling them into the car, and driving to church alone. The loneliness of early motherhood and the shaky ground of our marriage.

In the Visitation story, Elizabeth tells Mary that she is blessed for believing God's promise to her. Mary is no doubt scared and even incredulous. What had she said yes to? In the same way, a couple taking their marriage vows has no real sense of what they are doing. What did we say yes to?

Advent is a season, of course, about waiting. The church calendar includes Scripture readings and other prophecies—Old Testament stories about the Messiah, yes, but also apocalyptic readings about the end of the world. We wait for Jesus' birth and we wait for Jesus to come again.

And what is it that God has promised me, promised Josh? What promise am I holding on to? I don't believe it's necessarily a promise that our marriage will endure, or that Josh will be a Christian again, or that we will be protected from suffering. No—the promise I hold on to is that God loves me and will never leave or forsake me, come what may.

When Mary goes to visit Elizabeth, she goes because the angel of the Lord has just visited her and told her that her older cousin is also miraculously pregnant. Mary wants to see for herself. If Elizabeth is pregnant, then the angel of the Lord wasn't lying. If the angel of the Lord wasn't lying, then Mary can trust the promise made to her: that inside her virgin, teenage body, the Son of God is slowly being knit together. God the size of a poppy seed, the baby books might say.

When I read this part of the story, I find myself unexpectedly tender toward Elizabeth. Maybe it's because she shares my grandmother's and daughter's name, but I suspect it has more to do with how Elizabeth confirms Mary's story—the angel hadn't been a hallucination. Indeed, the Holy Spirit had been present in the clouds, forming the shape of a *V* over our heads, on the day Josh and I got married.

Because of Elizabeth, Mary can trust that God is indeed doing this marvelous, miraculous thing. When I am feeling low, I imagine Elizabeth beside me with her graying hair and round, pregnant belly. She reminds me not to be afraid, to trust that God was with us on our wedding day and is still with us now.

24

LIFE TOGETHER

y sister Sarah called to tell me her grade school sons
would be going to Honey Rock Camp the next summer—
the Bible camp I'd attended every summer from age nine
through high school, where I had met Caroline, and where I'd
worked as a wilderness trip leader in college.

Josh and I were sitting up late after the kids were in bed, de-
briefing the day in our living room. It was early June and everything felt sticky. Even my hair felt damp from the humidity. Josh
sat on the couch in his pajama pants, a laptop open.

"I just keep thinking about camp," I said. "I wonder how they
will like it."

"You're wondering how our kids would like it," corrected Josh.
We were sitting together on our worn-out couches, and I turned
to face him.

"Okay, maybe I am," I said. Josh closed his eyes and sighed.

"You know I never went to camp like you did," he said. I knew.
And I knew what he was going to say. I stood up quickly and
walked into the kitchen to grab a glass from the cupboard.

"Yeah and you would have loved it," I said, turning on the water faucet and filling up the glass. The sound temporarily shushed any outside noise, giving me a moment to think.

"I just don't want them to be emotionally manipulated or brainwashed," Josh said from the other room. I took a long gulp of water, then walked back into the living room.

"It's just that I don't know if I would be a Christian today if I hadn't gone to camp," I said, my throat tight. Shoot. Even I could hear the emotion in my voice. I didn't want to cry.

I took a breath, then another sip. All those nights out in the woods, all those Bible studies and altar calls. Yes, my faith has changed since then, but God was first real to me at camp. I was afraid that my kids wouldn't have any solid religious experiences. I wanted them to feel the warmth of a Christian community all around them as they explored the woods, sang hymns around a campfire, and portaged a canoe. I wanted them to trust Jesus with their lives and experience God for themselves.

"We don't have to decide this tonight," Josh said. He reached for my arm. He was right. Our daughter was only six, and it would be three more years before she was old enough for camp.

"It's not emotional manipulation if you believe it's true," I said, turning away.

When it comes to our kids and religion, Josh and I have mostly fought in hypotheticals. We agreed that the kids would come to church with me and go to Sunday school. The rest we muddle through. What about Vacation Bible School? (Josh was not for it.) How about Bible stories at bedtime? (I would read the Bible to them but not push it.) Should we pray before meals? (We compromised by singing a blessing.)

But camp—even hypothetical camp—was clearly touching a nerve in me.

It was the second day of a forty-eight-hour "solo" on Lake Superior's southern beach—the final challenge of a two-week-long wilderness trip that I was coleading for new students at Wheaton College. It was sort of like freshman orientation crossed with *Survivor*. After ten days of canoeing and hiking in the wilderness, twelve incoming freshmen were perched on individual rectangles of clear plastic—ground tarps that protected their sleeping bags from getting damp—and left alone for two days to fast and pray. Campers were strewn out in a long line along the shore—six to my right and six to my left—each one at a healthy distance from the next. There were no tents on solo, just ground tarps and sleeping bags, our ceiling the dramatic Northern Minnesota sky. Each camper in her own little hermitage.

Twice a day, my coleader, Alice, and I would walk between the campers along the shore and check on them. Speaking was discouraged—a thumbs up meant all was well. Some whispered that the fasting was making their bodies shaky, so I would slip them a graham cracker. Some whispered that they felt afraid, so I would squat down beside them to pray.

My lower half was nestled into a black-and-green sleeping bag, the cotton liner now bunched and twisted at the bottom.

The morning air was chilly, so I slipped my light blue fleece on over my shoulders. It smelled of campfire and must. I felt my hair as I pulled on the warm layer, which was thick with grease—it had been nearly twelve days since I had showered. I fished around in my sleeping bag for my winter hat, then slipped it onto my head to cover my dirty hair, which felt slightly damp from the morning dew.

There was light enough for reading, I decided, so I grabbed my Bible and opened it to the Psalms. Someone had shown me the trick of reading the Psalm of the corresponding day (for example, on August 16 read Psalm 16), so I read aloud my daily Psalm to the giant lake. "Lord, you alone are my portion and my cup; you make my lot secure. The boundary lines have fallen for me in pleasant places; surely I have a delightful inheritance."

I was an incoming college junior, just two years older than the campers, and this was my fifth time leading a wilderness trip that summer. The director of the High Road program asked me to come lead Vanguard, this trip for incoming students, and I said yes. The freshmen girls were classic overachievers, but most were far out of their comfort zones learning to use a compass or throw a bear-bag rope. One girl introduced herself as: "Amy. *A* stands for my average grade and my bra size." They were also spiritual overachievers and, like me, were brought up in church youth groups. They were pastors' daughters who knew their Scriptures. Students could get a credit or two for doing this course if they completed the required reflection paper once they were on campus. Some were using the solo time to start on their assignments, mostly to finish reading the assigned texts.

One of those texts was a slim book, almost pocket sized, by Dietrich Bonhoeffer called *Life Together: The Classic Exploration of Christian Community*. Over the past two weeks, the group had formed its own version of Christian community on the microlevel—a group of strangers learning to canoe and portage and to cook something called "texturized vegetable protein" over a campfire. There was plenty of time for things to get ugly—girls crying in the tents at night, girls snapping at each other for not packing up the bear bag before dark, girls crossing their arms and turning away from their navigation partner when it was clear we were lost.

My coleader, Alice, emerged from the woods carrying a toothbrush, a headlamp perched on her head, and wool socks tucked into Chaco sandals.

"Hey, have you read that?" I asked. I pointed to *Life Together*, which was peeking out of her wet bag, alongside a Bible and spiral journal.

"I have read it, but a while ago. I was going to look through it so we could debrief a little with the girls after the solo is over," she said. "Have you read it?"

"No," I said.

"Here," she replied, placing the slender book in my hands with a grin. "Read it this morning and then give it back. It's a game changer."

I picked up *Life Together* and started to read, pausing occasionally to copy down a sentence in my own journal. Dietrich Bonhoeffer wrote *Life Together* about his experiences in the Confessing Church, a small but devoted movement in Germany that opposed Hitler's regime and sought to subvert it. They had high ideals—they were standing up to a demagogue at great danger to themselves.

Yet as I read, I discovered that, though Bonhoeffer's group did stand up to Hitler, they struggled. If the Confessing Church had internal battles, was there any hope for the rest of us? Even Bonhoeffer's community didn't meet their mark. Bonhoeffer himself was executed after a failed attempt to assassinate Hitler.

The Confessing Church's movement sparked hope for those in the church who felt bewildered and disillusioned at their religious leaders' support for Nazism, and the war did end shortly after Bonhoeffer's death. Though he didn't kill Hitler, Bonhoeffer's writings continue to inspire millions to take unpopular and even dangerous stands for their ideals.

I scratched out one sentence in my messy handwriting, making a mental note to read it in our group debrief later: "The person who loves their dream of community will destroy community, but the person who loves those around them will create community."

When I told my friend Dana about our Bible camp impasse, she said, "Well, you don't want Josh to always be on the outside, do you?"

"What do you mean?" I asked.

"I mean, you already go to church on Sundays with the kids and he stays home, right?"

I nodded.

"So maybe the camp thing is just one more way he feels left out. Everybody in your family is doing Christian stuff except him. I'm not saying you shouldn't send them to camp. I know it's important to you. But you guys are your own little community, and everyone should feel like they belong in it."

I nodded again, even while my insides twisted with fear. I want our kids to love Jesus, to know God's presence when they paddle a canoe as I did. But maybe, in the long run, how Josh and I love and respect each other's beliefs will make a bigger impact on our kids' religious formation than whether they go to Bible camp.

In our marriage, neither of us carries executive authority. We argue and argue until, eventually, we find a solution we both can live with. Some days we can't hear each other or see it from the other person's perspective. I suspect we won't make a decision about camp until the registration deadline comes and forces us to compromise.

Until then, our family wilderness adventures are composed mostly of Saturday hikes in nearby Eloise Butler Wildflower Garden and Bird Sanctuary. We fill up a few water bottles, including the dented Klean Kanteen we got on our honeymoon, and throw some granola bars and bruised apples into a backpack. At the trailhead, we pick the route called Lady's Slipper Lane, which takes us on the boardwalk past native irises and cardinal flowers. Eliza skips ahead and Rowan uses a stick to poke every tree we pass.

As Josh stops to identify fungi growing on a downed log near our path, I remember Bonhoeffer's warning to love people more than my visions for life—whether that vision is for Christian community or the perfect religious upbringing for my kids. It's a struggle. I wonder if the work of love begins when our ideals shatter, when we're forced to sort through the broken pieces together.

The kids race past us on the woodchip trail, and we climb the hill to join the prairie loop. In a few months, the asters, goldenrods, and blazing stars will be in bloom. It's an ordinary thing, this family hike on a June day, but as we walk, I feel a surge in gratitude for our shared life together, this commitment to be a family where everyone belongs. At the top of the hill the kids jump out from behind a clump of trees to surprise us.

"I got you, I got you!" Rowan yells, delightedly, as Josh feigns shock. "Now you wait here," Rowan says.

"Don't come until we say so," Eliza adds before they run ahead and find a new place to hide down the trail. Josh and I smile at each other, waiting in our queue in their game.

Not all our big dreams for life together come true. But as my friend Kendra wrote recently, pieces of them absolutely do.

25

June 8

SAINT MARGARET MARY

*I*magine we are walking together through a convent that is being suppressed.

We are on the grounds of the Visitation School and Monastery in Mendota Heights, just a thirty-minute drive from North Minneapolis. The monastery buildings here are only fifty years old, but the community itself was founded in 1873, when six pioneering nuns made the journey on the Mississippi from Saint Louis to Saint Paul to start a new Catholic school for girls. When the monastic order outgrew its building in Saint Paul during the early 1960s, forty-five sisters (including a young Sister Katherine and Sister Mary Frances) made the move to the campus in the suburbs of Saint Paul. Some of the statues, paintings, and stained-glass windows came with them.

First, on the entrance drive, do you see it? It's a white, marble statue of Jesus opening his robes to uncover his chest. His gaze is cast downward, and he points to his heart, which is external

from his body. It's summer now, but I imagine his poor exposed heart gets covered in freezing rain and snow in winter months.

Now let's walk through the Visitation School main entrance. There, in that stained-glass window: that's Jesus with a red, pulsing heart wrapped in a crown of thorns and topped by a flame. Look down—there, a nun in full habit, kneeling before Jesus. Jesus is looking at her and pointing to his heart, which shoots golden rays that land on the nun's chest.

That's right: Jesus' blood-red heart is shooting out sunbeams like a sprinkler.

Here is the last one. Do you see a statue of a nun in full habit, holding a stone tablet with the same heart? That nun is Saint Margaret Mary Alacoque, a French Visitation sister from the seventeenth century, who had mystical visions of Jesus. She is the reason for all this strange religious art of Jesus touching his red, shining heart. The Sacred Heart devotion includes twelve promises, including one to "bless every house in which the picture of my heart shall be exposed and honored," which partly explains why images of the Sacred Heart are so common.

Sister Mary Frances once told me a story about teaching at the Visitation high school on the feast day of Saint Margaret Mary. She was walking through the campus and overheard the teenage girls making fun of the Sacred Heart.

"It was terrible," she told me. "To hear them laughing at this devotion, when it's all about God's desire for us."

The Sacred Heart is a tradition, or cult, rooted in Salesian spirituality. The devotion is about Jesus living in our hearts and of God being love. In his writing about prayer, Saint Francis de

Sales described it as "heart speaking to heart." (An alarming aside: Saint Jane de Chantal was so enamored by this idea that she branded the word "Jesus" on her chest with a hot iron. Saint Francis scolded her for it.) At its root, the Sacred Heart language sounds similar to language I encountered in evangelical churches. When I was a child, I was first saved by praying with my mother to ask Jesus into my heart. In church, we sang out to God to "open the eyes of my heart."

Devotion to the Sacred Heart has a long history in the church, but it was brought into the mainstream by mystic Saint Margaret Mary Alacoque. Though her image is all over the Visitation School and Monastery now, the sisters didn't believe Margaret Mary when she first reported her apparitions. For a year and a half, she had visions of Jesus and his heart. Her Mother Superior initially dismissed her stories as hallucinatory. But her confessor, Father Claude de la Colombière, believed her and verified her revelations, helping to popularize the devotional practices within the greater church. The Visitation became the first religious order to formally consecrate themselves to this devotion.

Margaret Mary's visions were popular, in part, because they countered a heresy that led many Catholics astray. The Jansenists promulgated a belief that humans were fundamentally unworthy of relationship with God. The bar for holiness was so impossibly high that Jansenists discouraged sinners from taking Communion, because who could possibly be pure enough to ingest the body and blood of Christ?

No doubt the Jansenists would have turned purple with rage at the thought of an unbeliever like Josh coming forward for

Communion, or even a doubting Protestant like me. But the Sacred Heart visions told Margaret Mary that God deeply loves flawed humans and wants to be loved by them. His heart was full of suffering and pain because so many stopped taking Eucharist. Margaret Mary's visions declared that God calls all to relationship with him.

In June I went to the monastery in my neighborhood for Mass on the feast day of the Sacred Heart. After reading about Margaret Mary's visions, I thought about my own mystical experience in the woods that past November. My marriage counselor seemed to think "spiritual singleness" could help empower me in my own religious beliefs and practices apart from Josh, but I was curious about what the nuns might think.

After Mass, as we gathered around the dining room table for muffins and toast, I asked Sister Katherine what she thought of the term "spiritual singleness." To my surprise, she said she didn't like it much.

"Being single, especially spiritually, doesn't resonate with my experience," she said.

Christianity, she told me, is meant to be experienced in community. It's not individuals who are the bride of Christ but the church. And monastics like herself, who live in such tight knit groups, have lived and practiced faith communally more than most.

I turned to Sister Karen and Sister Brenda to ask what they thought about "spiritual singleness."

"That doesn't resonate with me," said Sister Brenda.

"I don't really like it either," said Sister Karen, laughing and passing the muffin basket.

The nuns hate spiritual singleness. My mind was buzzing with questions, but soon Sister Suzanne tapped me on the shoulder and said, "It's time." I followed her down the steep basement stairs for the monthly Visitation Companions meeting.

As I settled into the couch and greeted the others, uncertainties hummed in the background, but my thoughts jolted back to the present when someone mentioned praying a novena.

"Novena?" I said. "What's that?" I always felt like I was playing catch-up as the Protestant in the room, muddling through saint's days and liturgies.

Novenas, Sister Susanne explained, are prayers said in cycles of nine. Nine is a holy number because it represents the ninth hour, the hour of Jesus' death on the cross. It's among the hours when monastics traditionally pause to pray during the daily office. The ninth hour is characterized by suffering.

Novenas are also associated with the Sacred Heart of Jesus, which includes a devotional practice to spend the first Friday of each month in adoration of the Blessed Sacrament (including attending Mass and receiving the Eucharist) for nine consecutive months. Those who complete the novena, according to the twelve promises of the Sacred Heart, "shall not die in [God's] displeasure." That promise sounds a lot like a formula for earning one's salvation. And yet, in an era where many were terrified of God's wrath and avoided taking Communion, I can see how God could use a promise of blessing from monthly

Eucharist as a channel of grace. We all want some reassurance, some certainty.

With all the confusion swirling around in my marriage right now, I want to latch on to the symbolism of nine with both hands. This is our ninth year of marriage. This is the year that I am trying to respect and uphold healthy boundaries, to pick the right battles and let others slide. So often this dance feels like suffering. But in and through all of this, I am dying to myself little by little. I am choosing love over fear; we are both fighting to hold on.

Saint Margaret Mary Alacoque's visions led her to a profound understanding of two things: accepting God's goodness and his cross. I wonder if that's my calling as well.

At Calvary on Sunday, I glimpse Margaret Mary sneaking up the stairs to the balcony. I follow the sounds of her shuffling footsteps. When I catch up to her, she is standing in the soft light that filters through tall stained-glass windows. There are no images of Jesus in these windows.

As I watch her, my mind returns to "spiritual singleness" and the way the Visitation Sisters so clearly did not connect with it. Maybe my mystic sister Margaret Mary can help me out. She was used to hearing from God in surprising and incongruous ways.

But Margaret Mary isn't looking at me. She's standing in front of the windows, and sunlight strikes her face and chest. I can almost hear Jesus speaking to her. *Come, see my heart. Come, know my love for you. Don't be afraid, but instead come and gaze upon my heart.*

Brené Brown uses the word *wholehearted* to describe people who live generously, with both vulnerability and resilience. Her research on wholehearted living includes ten markers, one of which is "cultivating intuition and trusting faith." Margaret Mary's visions of Jesus, his heart exposed, out there for anyone to see or touch, seemed to be describing the same thing.

"If you can't talk to God in prayer," wrote Saint Francis de Sales, "just let yourself be seen [by God]. Don't try too hard to do anything else."

Margaret Mary isn't going to turn to look at me, I know, but I stay on the balcony and watch her for a while. I realize suddenly that she is standing before these naked windows to let herself be seen. *Heart to heart.*

26

COMMON GRACE

*I*n early August, Josh and I attended a secular wedding. The couple got married at a natural history museum; their wedding ceremony in the planetarium. The bride was beautiful in a black dress and slicked-back blonde hair. The groom was handsome in a suit with a bow tie, his tattoos peeking over the cuff of his collar. They were trained scientists, like Josh, and all three had attended advanced chemistry classes together in graduate school. Her bouquet and the table centerpieces featured fungi. Before the ceremony, wedding guests were invited to browse the natural history collections, where they could handle animal bones and peer at frogs and snakes beyond plexiglass.

The wedding ceremony included a reading of a poem by Erasmus Darwin (the father of Charles), who wrote an awful lot about the erotic love of plants. Their minister, who was just a friend with a certificate from the internet, alluded to stardust, to how we are all made of the stuff—the elements—of the galaxy. Hydrogen. Oxygen. Carbon.

We sat in the planetarium and watched the couple exchange vows. I leaned into Josh's side as they promised to love one another, and when they kissed we cheered for them. Closing music started playing over the sound system, and it was one of my favorite songs by the Flaming Lips: "Do you realize / that everyone you know some day will die?"

In that moment, I couldn't think of anything more romantic. The inherent riskiness of a wedding never fails to take my breath away. If all goes well for these friends' marriage, it will still end in death. The Christian tradition teaches that marriage is a common grace for all people, even people who don't believe in God.

Watching these friends marry stirred up this common grace inside of me. Their love, commitment, fidelity, and honesty defied the warnings I had internalized that only marriages between Christian believers could be happy or successful. That Josh and my unequally yoked marriage was somehow synonymous with tragedy: a broken and frayed bond.

After we filed out of the planetarium auditorium, Josh and I held hands as we strolled through the museum, my high heels clacking down the hallway. We walked through galleries that contained simulations about the creation of the world from the tiniest of elements, bursting and blazing into being. We walked by a gigantic wooly mammoth and read placards about the ice age. So many fellow created beings have inhabited this planet, so many fellow created beings have died, recycling their bodies into the soil. Billions of prairie grass stalks have fallen to the ground. Birds have alighted in trees since the age of dinosaurs. Staring at the planets, reading the timelines that represent billions of years, trillions of sunrises and sunsets, so many summers and springs and winters.

We are so small and, as the psalmist wrote over two thousand years ago, "The life of mortals is like grass, they flourish like a flower of the field; the wind blows over it and it is gone, and its place remembers it no more." As we say on Ash Wednesday, from dust we were created and to dust we will return. Believers and nonbelievers both.

If all goes well for our marriage, it will end in death. Dust to dust. From nothing, to something, to nothing. Or, from elements, to creation, back to elements.

When Josh first deconverted, it felt like failure not to have "God at the center of our marriage" as all the Christian books had told us. But as time passes, I experience more and more the grace of our commitment, which has endured despite the ways we have both changed. I see all the ways we have sacrificed to make our marriage work.

When Josh and I got engaged nearly ten years ago, we held hands on a hiking trail at Afton State Park.

"I choose you," he told me. "Will you choose me?"

"I will," I said. I still do.

27

"I THINK I LOVE GOD"

*J*osh was steering the car around streets blocked off for summer construction, searching for a route through the suburbs to get us back home after visiting my parents. We were talking about a new book by Richard Rohr he had bought that morning, a book about spirituality.

"I decided to listen to a couple of podcasts with Richard Rohr—well, until my Bluetooth headphones died," he said.

"Were they any good?" I asked.

"Yeah," he said. "They were, actually. In one he talks about how many of us grow up with a more fundamentalist religion, and in the spiritual stages of development that can actually be a good thing because it gives us something to rebel against."

He went on to describe how Rohr acknowledged the religious diversity of the world, of how if one was born a Hindu in India then one would most likely be Hindu, or if one was born a Muslim in Egypt, chances are he or she would remain Muslim.

"He said that it's common for people to go through a period of deconstruction," he said. "And I know that's what I've been doing these last five years. But it's not a place where I want to stay forever."

I listened to him talk, my eyes scanning the traffic, my ears registering the hum of the air conditioner vents, my nose picking up hints of sunscreen and sweat from our children in the back, my tongue still carrying the aftertaste of decaf coffee. Or was it that way? Was I looking at him, or staring at the notifications on my phone, or counting the cars rushing past? I can never fully remember, though I do know there was a Styrofoam cup with black stripes in the center console, nearly full of decaf coffee.

Why is it so important to remember the details of this conversation—the early evening light stretching its legs, the green, leafy bonanza of summer in Minnesota, the coffee dangerously close to sloshing over the sides of its cup?

It's because of what he said next: "I think I love God."

I started blinking, my eyes suddenly prickly, and I turned to him. "What?"

His eyes didn't leave the road in front of him, though the corners of his mouth turned up slightly.

"Don't get too excited," he said. "I don't know what God is or how to define God." Then he turned to look at me and smiled. I smiled back, still blinking.

"Woah," I said, taking my hand to wipe my eyes. "Wow. I can't believe you just said that. That's amazing."

"Yeah," he said. "I mean, God is mystery. And I think I love the mystery."

We sat in silence for a while, staring at the road.

"Does this God love you back?" I asked.

"I don't know," he said. "I haven't gotten that far yet."

The next morning before church, when I was recounting this story to a close friend over the phone, she gasped. "I am so surprised," she said. "But having an agnostic who loves God is pretty great. As a Christian, I need to cultivate a greater love for God in my life."

I thought about how I had all but given up praying for Josh's conversion back to Christianity, not wanting to set myself up for disappointment, not really trusting that God would do anything about it. Why would God intervene in my piddling life when homeless people held signs at the intersections along Broadway Avenue near my house? God surely had more urgent matters to attend to—though I knew that wasn't quite it, either. The issue, really, was me: my lack of trust, my lack of belief, a sort-of functional agnosticism. My fear of being disappointed, masquerading as some bold commitment to Josh's freedom.

Flannery O'Connor wrote that faith comes and goes. "It rises and falls like the tides of an invisible ocean. If it is presumptuous to think that faith will stay with you forever, it is just as presumptuous to think that unbelief will."

Perhaps there are some Christians who are so close to God that their underlying belief and trust never wavers, their faith more like a steady body of water than rising and falling tides. I am not one of those Christians—I am more like O'Connor's shore, the tides of faith coming and going with some regularity. That Sunday morning after Josh declared his love for God, or mystery, I went to church. There were a few moments in that service, when I held the hands of my neighbors in the pews to sing our closing song, when the choir performed special music, when I cried and whispered thank-yous to God for showing up in Josh's life.

The associate pastor preached a sermon about how Jesus goes and hunts down that lost sheep. The pastor said, "That sheep isn't being led gently back by the shepherd in this situation. The shepherd is grabbing that sheep, picking it up, and hoisting it around his neck." The pastor moved her hands up to the tops of her shoulders, mimicking the motion. It looked like she had on an invisible neck pillow, the kind people wear on airplanes.

"That sheep is getting carried back," she had said.

I sat in church and prayed for Josh. I prayed the great Mystery would scoop him up like a lost lamb and carry him home. I prayed that a wave of faith would crash over us both, giving us an undeniable sense of God's presence.

28

NUNS AND NONES

*S*oon after Josh told me he might love God, I talked to my sister Sarah on the phone about a couple at our Presbyterian church growing up. They were the kind of church parents who went to all the graduation parties and chaperoned youth group trips.

"You know that Charles never actually came to church, though," my sister said.

"What?" I said. "But he was always there! At all the events!" I ticked off birthday dinners and bell choir concerts and church basement potlucks.

"Yes," she said. "He was always at the auxiliary church events but never in church services. He wasn't a Christian."

"Huh," I replied, racking my brain to try and remember if I had ever seen his black salt-and-pepper hair in the pews.

"Well, that's actually awesome," I said. This was a couple I had always looked up to for their hospitality. Maybe being in a mixed-faith marriage didn't have to mean losing our church community entirely, and yet, did Josh want that? Did he want to be an auxiliary church member?

It can't be easy, participating in a church community always from the outside. I wondered how Charles had made his peace with activities like driving kids to laser tag when he didn't believe in Jesus.

Still, it was enough to know it was possible.

Some couples have a permaculture gardening club. Others do home remodeling projects on the weekends and watch HGTV together on the sofa at night. Josh and me? Well, we'd had church.

In our first years in Minneapolis after graduation, our friends were mostly other young people that met for Sunday night dinners and Tuesday night prayer. Later, we started investing in an intergenerational community at a tiny Mennonite church in our South Minneapolis neighborhood. It's where Eliza was dedicated; it's where we brought refreshments to be served after the service and volunteered as greeters. We had potlucks and small groups and even were appointed as the young adult coordinators for a while.

But when Josh stopped coming to church, he also stopped hearing the announcements and the prayer requests from our Christian friends. Suddenly I was the sole carrier of the church community news. Then, when I left that church, we lost those familiar faces that had provided meals after our babies were born. We lost the community that still held the memory of when Josh and I were both Christians.

At Calvary, he showed up on occasion at fellowship hour, but he didn't want to stick around for long. "Just being here makes people think I'm a Christian," he told me, "and I'm not. It feels weird, like I have to explain myself." I was the one signing up to bring new parents a meal or marking the upcoming retreat on the calendar. Josh was on the outside, and we were no longer investing in the same community.

Instead, he found friends in other places: in graduate school, it was the Mycology Club; later, it was fellow teachers at the middle school where he taught earth science and the Mill City Running team. I had church with the kids on Sunday mornings; I now had the nuns and the Visitation Companions, but we didn't have much in the way of friends *in common*. During the week, it often felt as if we were just trading childcare—him, off to run on Wednesday nights; me, off to the monastery for morning prayer or church services. What place could we find where we both belonged?

Then, out of the blue, someone contacted me with the answer to all my problems. Katie Gordon is a leader of Nuns and Nones, a national initiative that brings together Catholic sisters and nonreligious seekers for dialogue and action. When we first talked on the phone, I scurried into my bedroom and turned on the white noise machine to block the sounds of my kids thumping up and down the stairs.

"Nuns and Nones is an experiment in community," she told me. "In some places, the group meets twice a month."

"Like a church," I said.

"Like a church for agnostics," she replied, laughing.

She explained the genesis of the project: In late 2016, a group of Dominican sisters had reached out to her in Grand Rapids,

Michigan, after she wrote an article about "the rise of the nones"—the growing trend of young people leaving institutional religion. There was interest in getting the two groups together to learn from one another. As it turned out, around the same time there was another gathering of Nuns and Nones at Harvard Divinity School, exploring similar questions.

Katie told me about the unlikely chemistry in the group she started in Grand Rapids: how after walking away from church, meeting the nuns had kindled a new spirituality inside of her. We traded stories about monasteries we'd visited; she taught me the difference between an apostolic versus monastic community of nuns. (Apostolic communities' primary charism is active ministry, such as administering schools or hospitals or serving the poor. The primary ministry of most monastic communities is their contemplative practice, like praying the daily office or adoration of the Eucharist.)

In the days afterward, my mind returned to our conversation again and again. A church for agnostics? Maybe that was something Josh and I could attend together.

I started dreaming about starting a new Nuns and Nones gathering in the Twin Cities. I imagined gray-haired Catholic sisters and tattooed twentysomethings sharing couches at the Saint Jane House. It was winter. A fire glowed in the fireplace as someone asked, "But how does centering prayer work anyway?" And I imagined Sister Karen explaining, "Don't be harsh with yourself when your mind drifts away from your intention. Every time you turn away from God is another opportunity to turn back toward God. See it that way. Each straying thought is a chance to turn back—to turn back to God."

"Is that what doubt is like?" I wanted to ask my imaginary gathering. "Is doubt something we needn't be mad at ourselves about? Is it just another time, another chance, to turn back to God?"

I imagined Josh in the room, my very own none sitting beside me. We rarely sat in a church pew like this, side-by-side, arms sometimes brushing against one another. Would this be a place where he would want to be? Where we could ask these big questions together? Would he hear my question about doubt and turn to me, his hazel-green eyes locking with mine and say: "Maybe every moment of doubt is another chance to turn back to mystery."

God. Mystery. Creator. These are all words for the divine. Could this be a place where we connect, find spiritual community? Would these discussions of spiritual practices enliven us both, sending us twirling around, spiraling inward, honing in to the great holy God?

I wanted to host a Nuns and Nones group like Katie, but first I needed to see what the Visitation Sisters thought of this plan. I sent an email about the idea to the nuns and told them I'd be at Wednesday morning Mass. I wanted to talk it through.

The kids rode their bicycles along the sidewalk down Fremont while I power walked, often giving a power shout "Stop! That's a driveway. Watch for cars!" We avoided orange cones and walked around sandpits where construction crews were building new curbs for the sidewalk entrances. I had coloring books and

My Little Ponies and a box of story cards in my bag, along with a puzzle we had borrowed from the monastery weeks ago and never returned.

I hoisted the kids' bikes up onto the front porch, the same porch where, nearly a year ago, I had first encountered the monastery on Halloween while trick-or-treating. Inside, Mass had already started, but Sister Brenda pulled out a chair, and I gathered Rowan on my lap and pulled out his superhero coloring book. Eliza sat next to me, old enough not to need placating every few seconds, old enough to listen to the strange words and ask me questions later. I remembered to pack a few graham crackers and, when it came time for the Lord's Supper, I passed one to Eliza and Rowan, as well as to the other little kids who'd come that morning. While the adults passed around the host in a golden dish, the children munched the sweet crackers.

During the passing of the peace, Rowan eagerly grasped the hands of the nearby nuns: Sister Mary Frances, Sister Katherine, even scooting between bodies to shake Sister Suzanne's outstretched hand.

"Peace of Jesus," Mary Frances said, her voice jolly and sincere.

After the priest announced, "the Mass has ended," I walked into the dining room where people crowded around the large rectangular table, helping themselves to coffee, muffins, and buttered toast with jam.

"Stina," Sister Karen said in her sweet, raspy voice. "Let's talk."

Sister Katherine sat beside us, and they told me how they had read my email aloud in the car the last night as they drove over to a dinner hosted at a neighboring parish.

"I am open to the Nuns and Nones idea, but to tell you the truth," Sister Karen said, "I kind of wonder what the point of this group will be. There seems to be so much misplaced energy in seeking out these practices from here and there." She reached her hand up as she said this, as if she were swatting away a fly.

Sister Katherine, no longer in earshot because of the noise in the room, turned to entertain Rowan, who was demanding more juice. He giggled as she made faces at him.

"Back in the '70s," Sister Karen continued, "I remember we tried this new liturgy in the Visitation Monastery in Saint Louis, and it was so complicated. I am glad we tried something new, but I was relieved that we could go back to something known, that we already knew was solid."

I nodded. It does take so much more energy to go out to pick and choose religious experience—to combine kabbalah beads and centering prayer with the occasional seder or technology sabbath. I wondered if Sister Karen was right, if Nuns and Nones was just another iteration of this impulse. Why not ground yourself in one tradition instead, one religion where someone has taken the guesswork out of things a bit? Here: this is the catechism; this is the daily lectionary reading. Here: these are the words of institution for the Eucharist. No need to improvise what has been said for two thousand years.

"But let the sisters talk about it," said Sister Karen, giving me a hug. "We need to decide together if this is something we want to try."

After we finished our toast, I said my goodbyes and began the walk home while the kids raced along on their bicycles. As I waited for the light to turn green at the intersection with Broadway, I thought about my none—my Josh. If a gathering was grounded in Christianity or Catholicism, then the assumption might be that one attending would share those core beliefs. I couldn't see Josh going for that. Why fake it? Why say "God" when you really mean "mystery"?

Sister Karen said that the sisters would have to talk about starting a Nuns and Nones community at their next business meeting. But even if the sisters hated the idea, I knew I couldn't let the idea die. Not yet.

29

NUNS' PICNIC

*T*he nuns tell me they want me to present on the Nuns and Nones idea at their September community meeting in a few weeks. There isn't much for me to do but wait.

Well. Wait, and finally introduce Josh to the nuns.

Sister Suzanne sent out an invitation to the spiritual formation group months ago, and I put it on our shared Google calendar. During the last week of August, the nuns host a picnic in a park for the Visitation Companions. When Josh and I talk through our end-of-summer plans, about whether we can squeeze in a camping trip to the North Shore of Lake Superior, I remind him of the picnic.

"We have to go," I say, pointing to the purple-shaded item on the calendar on my computer screen. "I committed months ago. And, you haven't really met the nuns yet."

Months later, when I ask Josh what he remembers about the picnic, he said he had a good time.

"You did?" I said. "I wasn't sure."

"Of course, I did," he said. "The sisters are so warm. They make you feel welcome right away."

It was true. The sisters seem to exude joy whenever I see them. Sister Katherine gives me a hug and a humongous smile, sometimes clapping her hands together in delight. Sister Karen leans in to ask me how the writing is going, how the children are doing in school. Sister Mary Frances's rich alto voice declares "Stina!" when she makes eye-contact, as though I were the prodigal daughter returning home. They are hard not to love.

The nuns' picnic is like this: wooden picnic benches in a park by the Mississippi River, a grove of towering cottonwood trees casting dappled shade on end-of-summer grass, kids running about the lawn, spinning, cartwheeling, leaping like little goats. The normal constraints of the city, the "watch out for the broken glass" and "hold my hand when you cross the street" are blissfully unnecessary. We are picnicking by the river and it is glorious.

I carry a bowl of salad for the potluck, two silver serving spoons poking out like bunny ears, and add it to a crowded table. Sister Suzanne bustles about, opening coolers and setting out plastic cutlery. The nuns gush and shake hands with Josh. ("So wonderful to finally meet you, Josh!") He makes small talk with the others. Someone hands us each a bottled water that sweats with water droplets.

Josh is with me, meeting the sisters and other Visitation Companions, and it's a good thing. We pile our plates with burgers, hot dogs, potato chips, salad, watermelon. My daughter sprawls across my lap, red juice dripping down her hands, listening to the adults chatter around her.

Someone has brought blue camp chairs, the kind that fold up like umbrellas, and my son sits with his paper plate on his lap.

Sister Karen offers him a small can of A&W root beer, and he takes tiny sips before carefully placing it back into the cupholder. We wear name tags and I meet new people, but mostly I watch Josh talking to the sisters, smiling. He laughs and they laugh, and later Sister Karen tells me, "You didn't tell us your husband was so handsome!"

At the end of the picnic, the sisters invite us to join them in evening prayer. They pass around booklets so worn and soft that I worry the stapled bindings will break, shedding whole pages across the lawn. We sing hymns and recite prayers and occasionally I shoot glances over to Josh, who is sitting at a picnic table on the edge of our circle, looking at his phone. The kids grumble, "This is boring," and I hand them potato chips, one by one.

We are a small circle, a cluster of Catholic sisters and lay-people, joining our words to an ancient prayer form. Josh sits on the outside edge, not participating. He is only here because of me, because of duty, because he knows our marriage only works when we try to love what the other loves. It's part of the commitment we have both made. When Josh was in the Mycology Club in graduate school, I would join his friends for forays to hunt for chanterelles and chicken-of-the-woods in forest preserves, not because I am crazy about mushrooms but because he was. Loving each other doesn't mean giving up our distinct beliefs or practices. Loving each other means we each seek to understand and honor what the other holds sacred.

In another way, it's how I practice the vows we made to mutually obey one another. Kathleen Norris writes that, at its root, "The word *obey* means 'hear.' And listening in that sense, as mutual obedience, is fundamental to marriage. . . . Such intimacy is a great gift, but it also contains the challenge of doing what is necessary, every single day, to maintain the relationship."

In all my thoughts on marriage growing up, I never expected that mine would lead to a nuns' picnic. I never expected to be here, praying thousand-year-old prayers while my husband scrolls Twitter at a respectful distance. But there is no denying the sweetness, the grins and laughter, the subtle flirting with these Catholic octogenarians who have taught me so much this year about faithfulness and joy. As I watched them, I remembered Kathleen Norris's statement to me the year before, when I had asked her about her own lapsed-Catholic husband: "Oh, he made friends with the monks while he was here." Maybe this is what she meant—that this overlap in worlds could feel like joy. That it reflected her husband's willingness to understand the things she found sacred.

When evening prayer finally ends, we gather up the kids who are now climbing trees. I place plastic wrap over the Pyrex bowl of half-eaten salad to take home. Sister Mary Frances offers the kids ice cream sandwiches that are melting into their paper wrappers, and their eyes light up like fireflies.

We say our goodbyes and carry our children across the grassy lawn to the parking lot. All the while, the Mississippi River is several hundred feet away, lazing its way down to Saint Anthony Falls where it will rush and pound and foam. I wonder how long it will take that water to travel the entire length of these United States, all the way to the Gulf of Mexico, where the fresh water releases into an ocean of salt.

In a month, Josh will run across this river on the Franklin Avenue Bridge a few miles downstream. He will be at mile nineteen of the Twin Cities Marathon, and the kids will make signs and stand with me along Summit Avenue to cheer for him. I don't understand why he runs marathons, why he wakes up at 4:30 a.m. to get his miles in before work, but I show up for his races anyway.

Wendell Berry writes that marriage, like any form, "serves us best when it works as an obstruction to baffle us and deflect our intended course. . . . The mind that is not baffled is not employed. The impeded stream is the one that sings."

Some days I am not sure where our stream is headed, whether there is a waterfall coming our way. Today, at least, we are listening closely to each other, circumventing rocks and meeting each other on the other side. Today, it sounds like laughter.

30

August 27

SAINT MONICA

*M*onica was the mother of the great North African theo-
logian Augustine. She is the patron saint of mothers,
alcoholics, conversion, and married women. The biographies
say she was married to a pagan man against her will and that he
was adulterous and violent. Her mother-in-law was also cantan-
kerous, and Monica felt lonely in her family as the sole Christian.
She was a virtuous woman and pestered her nonbelieving family
with her piety. Eventually, though, she wore them down, and
both her husband and mother-in-law converted.

She had three children who survived infancy. We don't
hear much about the other two kids and, truth be told, if
Augustine hadn't written *Confessions*—his doxological auto-
biography, still so devoutly read today—we wouldn't know
anything of Monica either. She is only known in connection
to her famous son, her sainthood conferred in connection to
his brilliance.

I first stumbled across Monica in a private Catholic Facebook group when a woman posted: "Please pray for my son to open his heart to Jesus again and come back to the church." In the thread that followed, others replied, "Amen," and "Saint Monica, pray for us!" and "For my husband as well." Someone posted a meme of a woman in a white robe staring piously up to the sky, a young man holding her hand and matching her gaze to the heavens. Across the image it read: "Behind a great man is persistent prayers of a mother for her son's great conversion."

Monica is indeed credited with converting Augustine to Christianity. While her son is off rollicking in hedonism and glibly praying, "O Lord, make me chaste, but not yet," Monica is stalking him across the Roman empire, prostrating herself at shrines and shedding buckets of tears. Augustine rebuffs her many times over. A bishop tells her, "The child of those tears shall never perish," which gives her the encouragement to keep going. Finally, after seventeen years of Monica's persistent prayer, Augustine is baptized into the church.

Monica reminds me of those unequally yoked books, which put the onus on Christian women to win their nonbelieving husbands back to Christ. They reference 1 Peter 3:1-2, which instructs women married to unbelievers to be persistent in good deeds so that their husbands might return to God. Why travel to a different country, these books assert, when one can be a missionary in one's own home?

After Augustine's hard-won conversion, Monica says she has no further earthly desires. Terrible husband? Converted. Terrible mother-in-law? Converted. Licentious son? Converted.

Now, her life's purpose is over. Handily enough, she is dead a few months later.

At first I didn't like Monica all that much. Maybe it's that I see myself in Monica—the deep sorrow, the desire for my husband to join me at church, the tendency to focus on other people's faith rather than my own. There is so much crying in Monica's story that rivers and streams are named after her tears. I imagine her clutching a hankie, hunched over at shrines, sobbing out petitions that God reach her beloved son. She is a spectacle, a caricature of the sacrificial woman, always concerned about the souls of others. When her son keeps ditching her, I want to take her by the shoulders and give a little shake, asking, "But what about your soul?"

It's not wrong to pray for someone's salvation, and I welcome any intercessions for Josh or me. But I am suspicious of Monica's persistence, her patience, and her relentless prayers. I am not so sure that's how conversion works, that the only missing ingredient from the lives of rapidly disaffiliating nones is a trusty rapid-fire prayer warrior behind the scenes. I know that my in-laws pray for Josh's conversion every day and that he is as uninterested in Jesus as ever.

"Give it time," the church ladies tell me, pulling me aside. "Josh might come around." I don't tell them that it feels dangerous to pray for his conversion outright, that I don't want to foster false hope. I don't want to be a missionary in my own home.

At Calvary, I imagine Saint Monica in the pew beside me with her box of Kleenex. The pastor invites people to offer a "praise, pain, or protest" to God while the offering plates are passed around. People stand up to share prayer concerns, and together we listen to a man describe his cancer treatments, to a woman's concern for her teenage son. Afterward, we stand and sing the doxology. When the whole congregation pauses for a moment of silent prayer, I see tears tumble down Monica's cheeks.

"Listen to your heartbeat," the pastor says. "Stand before God and quiet yourself. Offer up your own praise, pain, or protest. Call out for God to be God."

I squeeze my eyes shut, blocking Monica from my peripheral vision. In the silence, we stand side-by-side in God's presence. As she sniffles, I wipe away my own tears. *How embarrassing.*

In the Catholic tradition, people ask the saints in heaven to pray for them. They believe that saints, though long dead, are still interceding in that great cloud of witnesses that surround us all. This practice raises my Protestant hackles, but as I stand there with Saint Monica, I kind of get it.

It's clear that I don't always know how to pray for this—for Josh, for his faith, our faith—but I can ask Monica if she will. As we stand together, runny-eyed, she reaches over to squeeze my hand. I am grateful that she is at my side, crying in church with me and praying for us all.

31

INTERFAITH SUPPER CLUB

*D*uring the summer, we drove from Minnesota to North Carolina to visit family. We were in the car on our final day of the trip, the kids content for the time being, using new markers in new coloring books. For each state we passed through, my thoughtful mother-in-law had wrapped a small present for them to open. Virginia: little action figures. West Virginia: stuffed animals. Ohio: crayons and markers. Indiana: more stuffed animals.

"Are we in a new state yet?" Eliza asked from the back seat, kicking off her sandals.

"Still Indiana," Josh replied, catching my eye in the rearview mirror. It's 8 a.m. and we had about ten hours of driving still ahead, not counting bathroom breaks.

We had just pulled out of my friend Amy's gravel driveway in Upland, where we had spent the previous night. Amy had made us banh mi sandwiches with jalapeños for dinner, and her husband, Jack, had mixed us gin and tonics with fresh lime juice. After our long day in the car and fast-food lunch, I could have cried for gratefulness. A cluster of midsized cats ranged on their porch, some pawing on the glass repeatedly, trying to get inside. Eliza was in heaven, petting them, stroking their backs, snuggling their soft heads under her chin. After dinner, our kids played with theirs while we sat around their heavy dinner table. We asked Amy and Jack about life in rural Indiana. Pros: close-knit community, no traffic, a somewhat idyllic childhood for their kids. Cons: conservative politics, long winters, an hour's drive to Thai food.

"But tell Josh about your karaoke parties," I had said, nudging Amy with my foot. She laughed, then described the epic gatherings they sometimes hosted in the summer where friends and their kids would come and camp on their lawn, surrounded by cornfields. They would eat good food and drink wine. Kids would run wild together in and out of the house. The grown-ups would sit on the back porch and play hits from the '90s on their guitars. Everyone took turns using the karaoke machine in the basement.

"Yeah, the parties have been good," Amy said. "But we are ready to move on." Though they had made good friends nearby, they longed for life in a city.

We spent the night in their basement guestroom, and the next morning Amy was up early, brewing coffee and baking cinnamon-chip scones for us to wrap in napkins and take on the journey.

We drove along one-lane roads, passing abandoned barns and row after row of corn and soybeans. Occasionally we saw fenced-in corrals with horses or cows, and I would turn around and shake my city kids' feet: "Look, there are horses! Look, there are cows!"

"I know it has been hard for them to live out here," I said to Josh. "But those karaoke parties sound nice. I wonder if it's easier to cultivate community when you don't have as many options."

"Yeah, that could be," he said, keeping his eyes on the road. After our trip to North Carolina, where we had been surrounded by extended family, having time to talk one-on-one in the car felt nice.

"I want to build something together," I said, turning to face him. "Like a community that we would share. Friends that we have together. You have your running friends; I have my mom friends and church friends. It's not like we can just start a church small group or something." Josh flicked his eyes over to me, then reached over to hold my hand.

"Why couldn't we?" he said. "What about an interfaith group? Why can't we find other people who aren't all Christians to hang out with?"

"Are you being serious?" I said.

"Yes," he said. "What about Angie and Chris? They go to Calvary, right? Or at least she goes. I know he isn't a Christian. What about starting a small group with them?"

I took a bite out of my cinnamon-chip scone and tasted its buttery-sweetness on my tongue.

"That's a great idea," I said. Josh turned and looked at me, then lifted my hand to his lips for a kiss.

It was quiet for a moment, then Rowan cried from the back, "Are we done with Indiana?"

"Not yet," Josh and I both responded, in unison. There was still a long way to go.

September is church program kick-off season at Calvary. During the Sunday service, a host of speakers line up on the stage and take turns reading off opportunities for involvement while corresponding slides are projected on the wall to the right of the pulpit.

"Good morning Calvary," they all begin, and we all murmur "good morning" in response. This is the closest this American Baptist church will get to a communal liturgy.

The announcements tend to blur into each other:

"Good morning Calvary, mark your calendars for the upcoming men's retreat . . ."

"Good morning Calvary, volunteers are needed in the nursery . . ."

"Good morning Calvary, next week we are having a poetry and spoken word event . . ."

But when the new associate pastor stands up, I refocus.

"We are encouraging people to start small groups," she says.

I sit up straight in the last row and scan around the room. I can pick out the soft, brown back of Angie's head, I catch a glint of her cat-eye glasses when she turns her head. She is sitting next to her son, a long-limbed third grader named Max, who will soon scoot off with the rest of the grade school–age kids when they're dismissed for Sunday school. I don't really know her, only that she is married to Josh's friend Chris, who loves biking and isn't a Christian, either.

At the end of every service, Calvary has an endearing custom of singing a song together while everyone holds hands, swaying to the beat. Every week, I hold hands with somebody new, somebody whose name I often don't know. I am still new to this church and am relatively shy, ducking out after the benediction to collect my kids from the nursery. I lead my children by the hands to the refreshment table in the fellowship hall, the room thick with people chatting and hugging and laughing. I wave to familiar faces but keep my focus on my kids in front of me, who are now snatching handfuls of Ritz crackers from the plastic platter.

One child darts away while I am squatting down beside the other, explaining why one cookie was plenty. I see Angie across the room, but she is in deep conversation with someone. Once the children are settled with their snacks at a miniature table, I walk over to the welcome table that is stacked with flyers for how to set up an automatic ACH withdrawal to tithe to the church. There are sign-up sheets for the men's retreat but nothing about small groups.

My phone buzzes in my back pocket, and I duck into a corner to check my text messages.

It's from Josh: Done with my run. Want me to pick you up?

I turn my back to the room and type back: Yes. Now is good.

It had been over a month since I spoke with the Visitation Sisters about Nuns and Nones, and I still didn't know whether they were interested in starting a new group. The next day I was invited to meet with them at their weekly community meeting to talk about it further. I was not sure what to expect; Sister Karen hadn't been too keen on the idea back in August.

The meeting was at the Girard House and, after an opening Irish prayer, I was the first agenda item. To my surprise, the meeting went well; overall, the sisters like the idea of fostering more conversation with young adults about religion. They had questions about connecting with other Catholic sisters in the area, and I took careful notes so I could follow up to plan our first meeting, which we intended for early January.

When the meeting was over, I shut the glass door of the monastery and stepped out to the sidewalk, making my way to my coworking space on nearby Broadway Avenue. I inspected a Free Little Library and snagged a Magic Tree House book for my daughter, who had started reading chapter books in earnest.

As I walked along Fremont Ave., I thought back to a conversation I recently had with Josh. When I asked him if he'd like to attend a group like Nuns and Nones, he just shrugged.

"That's not something I'd sign up for," he said.

My contacts at the national Nuns and Nones movement admit that most of the millennials who are joining local groups are spiritual seekers or are interested in exploring and deepening their understanding of religion.

"Yeah, that's not Josh," I reply. He was on a religion break altogether. Just walking into a church with a deep crimson carpet or hearing the notes from an old Baptist hymn ("nothing but the blood of Jesus") triggered negative memories. Joining a small group of nuns for conversation, even with other agnostics, was not particularly appealing to him.

When one-third of millennials checked "none" on the most recent Pew Research study on religious identity, what did they mean by that? No one wants to be defined by something they are not. The research indicates that nones can be broken into three categories: atheists, agnostics, and "nothing in particular." Those who identify as "nothing in particular" are more likely to believe in some kind of God. They are more likely to be interested in hanging out with a group of elderly nuns, attracted to the stable rhythms of lives formed by one form of spirituality.

I am never quite sure where Josh is on the spectrum of belief, whether he is an agnostic, atheist, or a none. Some days he reads books by Richard Rohr and tells me he loves God, which he defines as mystery, or takes Communion at church. Most of the time, he is ambivalent. Uninterested. Unwilling to engage me in conversation about faith.

I kicked at a sample-size liquor bottle on the sidewalk. *There I go again*, I thought. *Getting invested in Nuns and Nones because I think Josh will be interested. Always trying to pull him along. Now I have to relinquish him all over again.*

When brought up in a tradition that explains salvation as intellectually agreeing about certain core tenets of orthodox Christian theology, is it any wonder that many young people have taken that literally? That it's either this or that, saved or unsaved, Christian or non-Christian, all depending on one's mental understanding of faith and its core tenets? When Josh could no longer intellectually agree to Christian beliefs, he was out of there. He lost so much. I have always been more comfortable with living in the gray.

I thought back to church yesterday. I thought about small groups, about Josh and our conversation driving through Indiana.

Maybe what we need is a place where we can just be who we are: an agnostic who sometimes takes Communion; a Christian who sometimes questions whether God exists. A place outside the walls of church where everyone in our family feels totally at home.

At work I shot off an email to Angie with the subject title "Interfaith family small group?"

Later, when the kids were in bed, I checked my smartphone: "I absolutely love this idea!" she wrote, then listed off a number of couples at church who are also in a Christian-to-none relationship. I didn't know any of them.

Our first Interfaith Supper Club is on a Sunday night, and I am playing the nervous hostess. It doesn't help that we never clean the bathrooms or vacuum the dust bunnies unless we have guests coming over. I whip up and down the stairs, carrying disinfectant spray and paper towels. I lug the vacuum cleaner in and out of bedrooms, cajoling the kids to put away their library books.

"You're making me tired," Josh said, lying on the couch. If he hadn't already washed the dishes and scrubbed the toilets, I might have snapped. "It doesn't have to be perfect."

"I know. It's just that we don't know these people," I reply, plopping down on the loveseat.

"You made delicious food for them," he said, standing up to stretch. "What's not to love?"

In a few hours, people arrive. I shake hands with Christian Julie and atheist Pete. I wave hello to agnostic Chris and give Christian Angie a hug, while their son, Max, wanders off to look at our bookshelves with my kids. I say "Welcome!" to agnostic/Jewish Jessie and Christian Savannah, offering to hang up their coats.

Everyone stands around, introducing themselves, while Josh and I move in and out of the kitchen carrying food. We dish up pumpkin chili and spinach salad with pears and candied walnuts. I stir the slow cooker with mulled cider, and Angie places a bottle of rum on the table beside it.

The kids are loud, and we decide to put on a movie for them in the other room while the grown-ups gather in a circle in the living room. We balance soup bowls on our knees; we scrape crumbly goat cheese with our forks.

I sit on the corner of the carpet and listen to people go around the room, sharing their own faith backgrounds. The how-we-met stories. The first-time-in-my-partner's-place-of-worship fiascos. I see couples that look like Josh and me. I hear stories that resonate: how our families of origin welcome or don't welcome our spouses, what we have learned from our partner's understanding of God (or lack thereof), how we struggle to find new rituals for our children.

We serve pie and coffee but run out of decaf. I sip my cider spiked with rum and feel the warmth spread down the full length of my body, tingling into my toes.

32

November 2

ALL SOULS' DAY

*F*or Halloween Eliza wanted to be Nightmare Moon from My Little Ponies. I can't do more than thread a needle, so I ordered a costume for her from Etsy and asked my mom to help craft a black and purple tulle skirt. Josh found a 3T Spiderman outfit at the thrift store, so we talked up the superhero costume to Rowan. It wasn't a hard sell.

I invited over old college classmates who lived nearby for soup and bread, followed by trick-or-treating in the Old Highland neighborhood. Halloween was on a Wednesday, in the middle of a hectic work week, and I scrambled to mince garlic and dice carrots while getting the children ready. I stirred pots of chicken with wild rice and savory ginger squash soups on the stove, then dashed to find compostable bowls and spoons from the cupboards, wipe down the bathroom sink, and pick up stray toys strewn about the floor. The kids raced around the house half dressed in their costumes, stopping every few minutes to ask if it was time to go trick-or-treating yet. Flustered, I sent them outside to set the picnic table with napkins, cups, and spoons.

As I opened the back door to let them out, I saw Josh pull into the driveway. He was driving our new used car we had bought earlier that day at the Brookdale Honda Dealership, where we had spent hours that morning sipping coffee from Styrofoam cups, eating soft M&M cookies, and signing dozens of papers I barely understood under fluorescent lights. Josh had just started a new job teaching high school science across town and biking to work was no longer an option. Our days were spent scrambling to figure out how he was getting to work, how I would get to work, and who would pick up the kids in our sole car.

Josh got out of the car and waved. I waved back, taking in the new red car. A few days later, at a staff meeting, I would tell my coworkers about the car. "Two cars! You are living the American dream," one of them teased. "We even have a gas grill," I replied, throwing up my hands in faux astonishment. We were a long way from our days living in an intentional community at Jubilee Partners.

"What can I do?" Josh asked, walking in the backdoor and laying down his orange backpack. He turned and gave me a kiss on the cheek.

"Nice car," I said, handing him a soup pot. "Carry this out to the picnic table? People should be here any minute."

We trooped in and out the back door, carrying bowls and pitchers of water, and the cat escaped into the yard. Soon our friends Brandi and Sam from college were knocking on the front door, their kids dressed adorably as green dragons. The other couple, Sonya and David, pulled in the driveway and out popped a toddler pirate wearing an impressive three-cornered hat.

The kids tromped through dead brown leaves in the yard while we ladled up bowls of soup and cajoled them to eat a little something before the glut of candy to come. I sat at the picnic bench, watching our friends with their children. Wiping mouths. Buttering bread. Calmly explaining why poking one's sister with sticks was not okay. We all graduated from the same evangelical college the same year, and within a few years we all married people we'd met there. Now, nearly ten years later, children wandered around us wearing superhero masks and fake black mustaches—*our* children.

I watched my friend Sonya hold her one-year-old baby and remembered when we were accountability partners in college, meeting to pray together and confess our sins in the fireside room of the student center. We first met on a mission trip to Honduras over spring break, a year before Josh and I would meet on a similar trip to Denver. I wasn't really sure what Sonya believed these days.

I wasn't sure what any of us believed. Out of the six adults, only three of us went to church semiregularly. To use the language we once spoke fluently ("God's will," "my walk with Jesus," "What I am learning spiritually right now?") now would have felt like dropping a poopy diaper in the middle of the picnic table. Instead, we swapped stories of childhood Halloweens. Some had spent them at trunk-or-treat parties. Others weren't allowed to dress up like ghosts or witches because a popular Christian radio program said they were demonic. Our parents had worked so hard to raise us in the faith, to protect us from the temptations of secular culture. Yet here we were, with our own children, happily participating in a holiday that celebrated ghosts, zombies, and spiderwebbed graveyards.

When it was time for trick-or-treating, we stacked the dishes in the kitchen and loaded into cars to drive a half mile down the street. David ran to a liquor store and met us later with a carafe of spiked hot cider for the parents to share. As we herded our kids from door to door, helping them climb up cement stairs and knock on painted doors, I wondered if our kids would attend church when they are our age.

"This is where the nuns live!" Eliza shouted, pointing to a large yellow house with a blue Peace sign in the front yard before charging up the steps in a blur of black and purple tulle.

Sister Katherine was there and ready with a smile. "Stina!" she said, giving me a hug, before oohing over my children's costumes and those of my friends' children. I smiled back at the familiar face. It had been just a year earlier that we had first met, on this very night. It had been colder and darker then, I remembered, and everything about the neighborhood unfamiliar.

The children held out their plastic jack-o-lanterns and the nuns dropped in several pieces of candy.

"Did you get my email?" Sister Suzanne asked me as she plunked Smarties and wrapped chocolates in shiny foil into their buckets. "I sent you an article. We'll discuss it when the Visitation Companions meet again soon."

"Yes, yes I got it," I said, leaning over to give her a side hug.

"We will also go over the final discernment retreat instruc-
tions," she said. "Make sure you schedule yours soon. And
remember the Advent commissioning."

I nodded and assured her that I was on it. The kids were
already out the door, so I gave my hasty goodbyes and slipped
out the front door after them. Josh was waiting on the sidewalk,
at the bottom of the stairs. I spotted my friend Randi and her
kids, who had already been out for nearly an hour and whose
candy bags looked heavy. She told me what streets they had
already hit, and which house was giving out bratwurst and beer
for the grown-ups.

I looked back at the monastery as the kids moved on to the
next house, bounding up its steps. Somehow I had imagined this
moment to be different. Here we were, on the anniversary of
meeting the nuns, and I wanted it to be profound somehow.
Would I see the saints I had journeyed with over the past twelve
months among the trick-or-treaters on the street? Jane, with her
commitment to God after forgiving her husband's killer; Elisabeth, with her private spirituality and confidence in God's
promises; Margaret Mary, with her mystical knowledge of Jesus'
sacred heart; or Monica, with her trail of tissues and faithful
prayers? I wanted to be able to look back on the year and see
some kind of tangible change, to see how journeying with these
mystical sisters had transformed my faith.

Instead my attention snapped back to reality—to Rowan,
who was calling my name. He needed help picking up spilled
candy. Eliza was already a house ahead, and I yelled after her,
"Slow down, wait for us!" while Josh trotted after her to catch up.

Our friends stood nearby, and I needed to ask thoughtful questions about their work, about their plans for Thanksgiving.

There was nothing profound about it. I didn't see the saints darting in and out of my peripheral vision; I didn't imagine them dwelling in the homes that we visited. I was caught back up in the daily scramble of family life. Yet I sensed God with us even here, and I knew I wasn't alone.

We approached a street and crossed it together, the grown-ups holding the hands of the kids in a long daisy chain.

While some Protestants host harvest parties in church basements, Catholics celebrate the fall holy days of All Hallows Eve, All Saints' Day, and All Souls' Day, a trio of remembrances for those who have gone before us. At my children's Spanish-English dual-language preschool, they celebrate the Day of the Dead and even set up a little altar in the hallway between the classrooms so students can prop up photos of dead relatives to remember. At home, we play the movie *Coco*'s soundtrack and talk openly about death, about how when we die, we return to be with God.

At a staff meeting two days later, on the Feast of All Souls, my Catholic coworker Jessie asked us to bring a photo of a dead loved one, then to share a little about that person. At the end of our time of sharing, each person would say the dead person's name, then the rest of the staff members would respond, "Pray for us."

I spoke the name of my Swedish Lutheran mormor, Connie, and my German Mennonite grandmother, Elizabeth. I wonder if they turned a little in their graves when our crew of Catholics and Protestants called on them to pray for us. The traditional Catholic understanding of the communion of saints, where we can continue to pray with and for the dead, is that the veil between life and death is thinner than we suppose.

I ran across an article online by someone called "Super Saved Catholic Dave," who lays out a scriptural foundation for this practice and draws on the earliest Christian writers—Origen, Saint Cyprian, Saint Jerome—as believing in the intercession of saints and angels. I read another article by the archbishop of St. Louis, who writes that the dead can "accompany us on our individual spiritual journeys" and can "communicate with us along the way."

This makes more sense to me, especially as I turn to my Catholic prayer book and read about the saints' lives. They speak to me now through their biographies and writings. I sometimes hear Saint Francis de Sales's words in my ears when I oversleep or snap at my husband: "Be gentle, be gentle with yourself." Sometimes I speak back, "Got it, Francis."

Over Thanksgiving, my in-laws come to visit. We set up a makeshift bedroom with a sliding curtain that partitions their space off from the front living room. Since they can't close a door, our children often crawl in their bed early in the morning for snuggles and to read books. My in-laws claim they don't mind. Josh and I believe them, relishing the extra hour of sleep in the morning.

My in-laws are early risers and have a daily practice of prayer and reading their devotional books and Bibles. I come downstairs, still in my pajamas, and my mother-in-law is reading the children's Bible to Eliza. Later, my daughter draws pictures of Jesus and writes words like "faith," "love," and "hope," and presents them to me proudly.

The holiday goes smoothly; we roast a Thanksgiving chicken and make yeast rolls using Mamaw's recipe. We go for walks along Cedar Lake Trail and spend hours raking up leaves in the backyard. My in-laws are the easiest of houseguests (they wash dishes! make dinner! help fold laundry!) and laugh easily, goofing off with the children. I don't want them to leave.

But after we drop them at the airport, Josh confesses to me that it happened again.

"My dad said that he is sad because we won't be spending eternity together," Josh says.

"He said that?" I respond, plopping down on the couch beside him and taking his hand.

"Yeah. When you guys were in the other room, he asked to have a conversation. I knew that the visit was going too well. I knew something like this was coming."

"Wow," I say, "I am so sorry." We sit there, side-by-side, in silence.

The words roll around in my head: *Not spending eternity together.* I know they are doing their best to love Josh, that these awkward conversations come from a sincere place. But how much fear must be nestled in their hearts, a real fear that their son is going to hell and will be separated from God, forever?

"We are praying for Josh every day," my mother-in-law had told me when we were peeling potatoes into long skinny spirals on Thanksgiving morning. "We're grateful that you are bringing the kids to church."

I nodded, then changed the subject.

I wished they wouldn't try to convert Josh, even if I understood their fear. I'd felt the same fear prickling in my throat when I spoke with atheists on the Camino or when I invited my non-believing peers to youth group in high school. At Bible camp, I shared my testimony on wilderness trips, trying to fit my faith experience into a conversion narrative that would appeal to my campers. Just accept Jesus into your heart, and your life will be transformed. I feel that fear even now, somedays, when I wonder if my own kids will be Christians when they grow up.

Faith in my thirties has been unpredictable—one that doesn't fit into a tidy before-and-after salvation testimony—and my evangelical impulses have faded along with my certainty. I believe that God never relents in loving and reconciling all things, even as I struggle with unanswered questions around heaven, hell, and salvation. And on the days I doubt even that, I call on my mystical sisterhood of saints—my Jane, Elisabeth, Margaret Mary, and Monica—to pray for us all.

33

BECOMING A COMPANION

There was something about how the orangy-red maple leaves had collapsed in the backyard, as if the tree had slipped out of her skirt, that made me wistful. It was December already, a year past that first Wednesday morning Mass when Sister Suzanne told me she'd brushed her teeth beside Dorothy Day. For a year now, I had been meeting with Kristin and Jane and Kathie every month to talk about Salesian spirituality and share from our lives.

It was time, now, for the final retreat to discern whether I should make a commitment to become a Visitation Companion. One Saturday morning, I joined the sisters for prayer in the small chapel at the Fremont Avenue house. Another woman I did not know was also in the chapel, along with Sisters Karen and Suzanne and Mary Frances. Sister Brenda handed me a set of books: a hymnal, a book of antiphons, and a book of Psalms, with a laminated Song of Zechariah acting as a bookmark.

Though I had prayed with the sisters in this tiny chapel many times over the year, I still got lost moving back and forth between the prayer books and Psalms and blue hymnal. The opening prayer was sung: "Oh Lord, open my lips and my mouth shall proclaim your praise!" We sang antiphons. Each side of the chapel took turns chanting the stanzas of the Psalms, back and forth, sing-chanting the ancient words of David.

Later, when I read an introductory book on Catholic theology, I would come to understand the meaning behind many of the things done during Mass: the reverential way the sisters would cross over their foreheads, mouths, and hearts before hearing the Gospel read out loud; the emphasis on communal readings of Scripture, knowing full well that Christians need community to properly engage the sacred texts.

During the time set aside to offer up our own petitions, the woman I didn't know asked for prayer for her husband. "Pray for him," she asked as tears shone in her eyes, "pray for our marriage, which feels so fragile. Thank you for being my spiritual community, my sisters."

After, I climbed the stairs to a little, tucked-away bedroom on the third floor of the house. The novitiate. I dropped my backpack on the floor. On the walls were pictures of different artists' renditions of the Visitation story. The stairs were steep and creaked underfoot. It was cold inside the house. I dragged in a space heater that had been left in the makeshift chapel and plugged it in, its grill glowing red.

There, I did the assigned reading and went through the retreat questions. I've agonized over many decisions in my life—what college to apply to, whether to get married, what job to pursue. But this? Did I want to be a Visitation Companion? This wasn't hard. Unlike Sister Katherine's discernment story, I didn't need a priest to flip a coin to tell me what I wanted.

Yes, my heart said clearly. Yes, yes, yes.

When my retreat was over, I set up a meeting with Jody to talk it through. We met at Breaking Bread, a café that serves soul food midway between my house and the monastery. Over biscuit sandwiches and portabella mushroom cakes, she asked me how it went. I said that it seemed right, almost natural, to become a Visitation Companion. That I hadn't been so sure at the start of the formation process, but now I knew that I wanted to take this next step. The only thing that I wasn't quite sure of was my ability to commit to doing extra service during the year ahead. I was working nearly full-time, writing a book, raising small children, and it was harder to get away in the evenings. Was I, in good faith, becoming a Companion when I didn't have much margin in my life?

"I felt some of that pressure in my earlier years," Jody told me. "But now I understand more that being a Companion is mostly about carrying the charism of the Visitation with you. It's mostly about practicing Salesian spirituality wherever you are."

I took a sip of coffee and remembered Saint Francis de Sales's maxim, "Be who you are and be that well." The charism, or spirit, of the order was to live faithfully in one's humdrum life, to give each day over to God, expecting difficulty and obstacles along the journey.

"And, don't forget that the sisters really want you to pray with them," she said. "Praying with them regularly is a great way to show your commitment to be a Visitation Companion."

It seemed too easy. Stop trying to practice your faith alone, just show up and sing Psalms and hymns and listen to the Gospel being read. This, too, is a ministry. This, too, is companionship.

On a cold Saturday morning in early Advent, I joined Kathie and Jane and Kristin at the commissioning service for Visitation Companions. The ceremony came at the end of an Advent retreat at the monastery, and a group of around twenty-five people were there to witness our promises.

Jody handed out three items: a loaf of homemade bread, a book about Salesian spirituality, and a small oval medal on a long red ribbon. On one side was the face of Saint Francis de Sales; on the other was Saint Jane de Chantal. She handed these items to me, but not before I was invited to share my intentions, my hopes for the year of partnering with the monastery in prayer, study, and service.

I was not prepared—I didn't know I would be making this statement, so I blurted out how I found the nuns while trick-or-treating, that I knew this could be a place where I belonged. That it was here that I wanted to explore spiritual singleness, and it was here that I realized that I am not single at all.

Then the crowd, all smiling faces pointed at me, clapped loudly, and Jody handed me the book, the bread, the medal. I put Saint Francis and Saint Jane around my neck and beamed. I touched the small emblem at my throat and stepped back to hear from the others making their intentions that morning.

That's what they were: intentions, not vows. I was not becoming a nun but instead joining the sisters in their ministry of prayer and presence. Josh and the kids weren't there to witness my intentions, but I knew they supported my commitment to this spiritual community. I was becoming a Companion.

After the Interfaith Supper Club's first few gatherings, Sunday mornings at Calvary felt different. When I walked into the back of the sanctuary, Angie waved me over to sit with her. I spotted Julie with her newborn son, who was born on Epiphany, and gave her a hug. I got to hold the baby and smell his head. Jessie and Savannah sat together near the front of the sanctuary, and I made a mental note to find them after the service and ask how their wedding planning was going.

On Christmas and Easter, Chris and Pete are there, too, and Josh is by my side. He leans over when the choir starts to sing "Our God Is an Awesome God" and whispers, "This song is too much, I need to go take a walk," and I whisper back: "Okay." As he slides out of the pew and walks to the back of the sanctuary, I glance over at the other couples. Pete is subtly looking at his phone. Chris took a bathroom break a while ago. Jessie is nestled next to Savannah but doesn't sing.

God bless them all, I think, *God bless all of these agnostic or atheist or otherwise spiritually ambiguous partners. They are only here out of love.*

Sometimes we all sit together in a pew, all us interfaith families, and I remember seeing the seven Visitation Sisters taking up a pew of their own during Sister Brenda's first vows, like seven beads on a string. It makes more sense, now, why Sister Katherine and the rest hate the term "spiritually single." Christianity isn't meant to be practiced alone.

After two years, I can't claim to be new to Calvary anymore, or the monastery for that matter. Now I am on the lookout for other singles who tread water during fellowship hour.

I don't imagine the saints as often in the pews these days, but I do still walk over to pray with the nuns when I can. On those mornings I learn about another new saint's feast day and hear the sisters reflect on their mystical lives.

When I sing the doxology with the congregation at Calvary, I sometimes look around at the nuclear families and singles and couples in the pews. I hear their voices all around me. I am not alone; I have never been alone.

34

February 8

MORNING PRAYER

*N*ow that I am a Visitation Companion, I try to make it to the monastery for morning prayer. Even when I slip in and out of certainty about my own faith, I always feel better when I pray with the sisters.

"O Lord, open my lips, and my mouth shall proclaim your praise" the sisters sing most mornings in the tiny chapel on Fremont Avenue. Today, despite last night's snowfall, I am determined to join them. After opening the back door into a drift of new snow and wading out to the driveway in my Sorrel boots, I struggled to clear the car windshield of its bumpy ice.

By the time I finished and arrived to the monastery, I was fifteen minutes late. I climbed the cement steps, which someone had nicely shoveled earlier in the morning. Was it the men in transitional housing, who helped the sisters with seasonal chores? Those men had helped carry in the nuns' Christmas tree and carted away furniture no longer needed. I wondered whether Sister Brenda had been out in the snow that morning yet. As the Texas-raised former Baptist missionary to Asia, she had a delightful tradition of making snow angels in the backyard—one for each sister—whenever there was a fresh snow.

The snow was so bright that I had to squint. I picked up the *Star Tribune*, which lay in its plastic sack on the front stoop, and carried it inside the covered front porch. The front door was locked. As I knocked, I could hear the electric keyboard begin the opening prayer, "Oh Lord, open my lips and my mouth shall proclaim your praise."

I was surprised—and a bit relieved—to hear they were getting a late start. After a year of praying here, the words were familiar to me. Sometimes they would spring up, while washing dishes or walking to the mailbox, and I would hear those notes ringing in my head. For now I stood and listened, the sunlight gleaming through the porch windows, the brilliant cold air moving in and out of my lungs in cloudy breaths. I knocked again, then stopped.

It was a holy moment, standing outside a locked door, listening to the voices of women singing, the cold sharpening each of my senses. The Jack Frost–latticed ice crystals on glass, the new snow and the smell of stacked firewood, the feeling of cold on my face, my fingers, my toes. As I stood there, I remembered that holy moment last November, when I got lost wandering in the Massachusetts woods. The words "spiritual singleness" had appeared, ex nihilo, and set me on this journey. And now I stood here at the monastery's front door, just waiting, knowing that I wouldn't be there long, that soon there would be a pause before the first antiphon. I would again rap my knuckles on the glass, and someone would hear me and open the door into spiritual community.

A woman around my age came to the door. I had met her a few times at Mass in the summer. She was with her husband and two small kids, and they sat clustered around the piano bench where Sister Mary Frances sat behind the keyboard. When I walked into the small chapel, Sister Karen pointed to a vacant chair they'd saved for me. It was Sister Mary Virginia's chair—she had broken her hip a few weeks ago and was unable to come to morning prayer.

I took the seat—Mary Virginia's seat—and felt my own spiritual poverty. Despite everything, the sisters welcomed me to sit as an equal, to be among the choir, to sing antiphons and pass around the golden bowl of Communion wafers.

As I took my place in the chapel, I knew that I was welcome here, even though it's not my home. There are kids present, but they're not my kids. I am not a sister, not covenanted to this community. My vows were made to Josh, my promises to have and to hold. He is at home, making breakfast for our own children, washing last night's dishes. I am here to foster my own spiritual identity, to practice my faith and learn from these companions, so I can return to my family and love them well.

I picked up the prayer book with the morning's antiphons and flipped to the front cover. The book was published in the mid-1970s, and there, in delicate cursive that reminded me of my grandmother's writing, was the name Sister Mary Regina.

When I asked Sister Katherine about it later, she said the monastery holds on to the prayer books of sisters who have since passed for visitors to use. When I told her my book had Sister Mary Regina's name, she closed her eyes for a moment. "She was a real leader in our community," she said. "I miss her. We were very close."

I examined the book more closely as we prayed through the Psalms and sang hymns and antiphons. The pages were soft and rounded at the edges, the spine cracked from decades of daily use. Each page bore pencil marks from where this now-dead sister had written chant breaks. I sensed the pages themselves were soaked in her prayer.

After the Scripture readings, there was silence. One sister spoke, "The Psalm today makes me think about what's happening on the border." Most monastic communities do not encourage individuals to add their own commentary in the midst of morning prayer, and I suppose that if a person was in a larger community then the practice might not work. But these sisters are intimate. They see their charism as primarily relational, a reflection of the biblical Mary and Elizabeth, two women that bless each other and bear witness to God's work in the world.

The little kids moved back and forth between Sister Mary Frances and Sister Katherine, who held them on their laps. Midway through Psalm 147 ("when the world is like ice"), Sister Brenda's phone pinged. She lifted up the screen, which was open to the Lyft app. In a few minutes, she motioned to Sister Mary Paula, and they made a hasty exit, followed by Sister Mary Frances.

Sister Karen explained. "Sorry for the interruptions this morning—we've had to push back prayer and it conflicts with some meetings, so everything is a little messed up." Then she launched back into the prayers of intercession.

Later, when Sister Katherine and I sat by the fire, she reflected on morning prayer. In the year I have known the Visitation Sisters, they have experienced big changes. They watched their sister convent close and welcomed a new member, Sister Mary Paula, from that monastery into their community. Despite all that transition, they continued in their ancient rhythms, gathering to chant Psalms from old books saturated in faithful prayer.

"But that's just the way things are, and it's what makes Salesian spirituality work so well," Sister Katherine said. "You hold on to the schedule, but you have to be flexible. You have to go with the interruptions and changes of plans. And who knows how the Spirit will show up next?"

She took a bite of jelly toast before going on. "I can't remember Saint Francis de Sales's exact words on this, but he said that a pliable heart will not break."

A pliable heart. Not completely malleable, like playdough. That would hold no center, no sense of itself. But *pliable* connotes something firm but bendy—like the wand in Mr. Olliander's shop that is eventually matched with Harry Potter. Marriage requires a pliable heart, a willingness to bend, to yield to the other, to see God in the interruptions.

"O Lord, open my lips," I sing with my not-sisters, longing for the man wrestling with our kids on the living room rug, the one who brings me coffee each morning without fail. I want him to be my *anam cara*—soul friend. I want to be one in spirit.

We will likely never share a religion again, but our vows together still hold, and so does our love for one another. Our children are our common, daily work during this season of life, the ones we nurture and guide and hold close. Each day, we build a home for them to know safety and love.

"O Lord, open my lips," the nuns are praying most mornings when I am home instead, boiling eggs, buttering toast. We don't recite the Liturgy of the Hours or even pray together much in our agnostic-Christian home. We have other rhythms: family meals, school and work, weekend hikes, movie nights. In between our sacred daily work, we talk—sharing our own commentary in another ordinary day.

I know that many people are praying for us. Our parents, the Visitation Sisters, my church community at Calvary.

I am grateful for their prayers, but I no longer feel fear's tightness in my chest. I am learning to take deep breaths, to trust Josh's eternal fate to a greater power than I possess. "O Lord, open my lips," I hum to myself each morning, unable to keep myself from praising a God who opens his sacred heart to agnostics and doubters alike.

In the first years after Josh's deconversion, I would whisper to the Holy Spirit: "This is on you to woo him back." Now, after walking with the Benedictines and Visitation Sisters, I rest in Sister Theresa's wisdom that everyone is on a journey with God, whether they know it or not. Josh most likely will never be a Christian again. And if God is really good, I can still trust God to be good after death.

I don't tell my children that Josh is going to hell because he is no longer a Christian. I don't want them to feel the way I did in elementary school, when I sat down my best friend at the back of the school bus and tried to convert her to Christianity. I don't want my kids to live with the fear that God might forever cut him off from his family in the afterlife.

I wear the image of Saint Francis de Sales on a little medallion around my neck. Francis, the patron saint of writers, wrote a voluminous treatise on the love of God. But Francis didn't always know God's love. He lived for several years in morbid terror of losing his own salvation. Francis worried that he was not among the elect. You were either in or out. Saved or damned. But how could you know?

This question sent de Sales into a flurry of existential angst. After months of torment, de Sales stumbled into a church and knelt before a statue of the Black Madonna. There he prayed the Memorare and declared that, in fact, he didn't care one whit if he was saved or damned. It was enough to live for God this day, to choose the everlasting water of life in the present moment. Even if he was going to hell, Francis de Sales was still going to live for God.

A strange and sweeping peace rushed over his soul, putting out the fires of anguish that had tormented him. And from that day forward, Saint Francis began proclaiming the love of God as a missionary—but it wasn't unreached people groups that he converted. He targeted Calvinists, Protestant Christians, the ones living under the predestination theology that had once terrified him, and he spoke to them about the all-encompassing love of God. Saint Francis saw humans as inherently good. He warned fellow Christians against focusing unduly on hell and damnation but instead preached a message of hope, of comfort, of joy. His theology didn't traffic in fear but in trust that God is good.

When I dig into my limited understanding of salvation, I find comfort in Francis's decision to stop focusing on what happens after death and instead live for God today. I don't have to live in dread every day of my married life. These are the truths I hold close: that perfect love drives out fear. That nothing can separate us from the love of God. That God is good. That God is bigger and better and more mysterious than we can comprehend.

A few years ago, I attended a writing conference where I heard Lutheran pastor Nadia Bolz-Weber give a blessing over the audience:

"Blessed are the agnostics," she said, riffing on the Beatitudes while extending her muscular, tattooed arms over us. "Blessed are they who doubt. Those who aren't sure, who can still be surprised. . . . Blessed are they for whom death is not an abstraction. Blessed are they who have buried their loved ones, for whom tears could fill an ocean."

As she spoke, I felt those blessings covering us all: the in-laws who worry about their child's soul after death, the alienated son who no longer believes. It even covers me, the one who doubts, who isn't sure, but is still hanging on to faith by her fingernails.

Maybe we will all someday be surprised. Maybe my in-laws' prayers will be answered, and Josh will return to faith in Christ. Maybe our twenty-first-century understanding of heaven and hell will be different from our actual experience of death. Maybe God's love reaches nonbelievers in ways and through channels we don't yet comprehend.

I hope we are surprised. All of us.

AFTERWORD

Nuns and Nones a Year Later

*O*ctober 1, 2019

After a few more conversations with the Visitation Sisters, we finally held the first Nuns and Nones gathering on a dark, below-zero evening in January. That night, like magic, a mix of millennials and monastics showed up at the Saint Jane House in North Minneapolis. We slipped off our shoes at the door and hung up our coats, ready for intergenerational conversation about faith and activism. Some of the young adults were religious, others weren't, but all sought a place for spiritual conversation where prescribed beliefs aren't an expectation.

Sister Katherine and I have been cofacilitating the group for nearly a year now, and other sister-millennial pairs are stepping up to shape the topics and discussions we share together. We talk about common stereotypes of nuns and millennials, about the ways we have been hurt or healed by institutional religion.

Sister Brenda is also a regular, along with a handful of Catholic sisters from other religious orders in the Twin Cities.

Sister Brenda recently told me that the Visitation Monastery is like a medieval anchor-hold—a place for people to seek and find spiritual community and wisdom. What brings the millennial seekers to Nuns and Nones, I suspect, is the sisters' solid footing in the Catholic tradition: those years upon years of formation, reading the daily Scriptures, taking Eucharist, greeting each stranger as Christ at their front doors. Our gatherings are a place for spiritual hitchhikers to find stability and hone inward, like a spiral, returning again and again to God.

At a recent Nuns and Nones gathering we watched a documentary called *Radical Grace* about the "Nuns on the Bus," who were censured by the Vatican for being politically active in support of the Affordable Care Act. After the film we sat in a circle to debrief. Several of the millennials noted the nuns' courage in standing up to Papal authority. Sister Mary Frances— the Visitation sister who helped the monastery in Mendota Heights die a good death—cleared her throat, a plate of tortilla chips and salsa balanced on her knees.

"You women are the future of the church," she said, addressing the six millennial women who were present. "You may not become Catholic sisters, or even attend church, but you do have big shoes to fill. We need you to carry the charism, the spirit, of this work forward."

I looked around at the other young women in the room. We were not well organized. We had not taken vows to one another. I thought about my experiment in the new monastic movement,

and of the community houses of young, idealistic Christians who tried and failed to live prophetically together. How would we possibly carry forward the sisters' charism to love in the face of adversity? How could we model a gentle yet steely, relational spirituality?

There is no filling the shoes of a Catholic sister—period. But if there is one thing I've learned these last two years, it's that even monastic women do not live their faith on their own. The Visitation Sisters have taught me that God is known by honoring our enduring commitments to love the people around us, even when monasteries close. Even when your spouse changes religions. That faith is lived by choosing virtues, both small and large, each and every day.

Josh doesn't come to Nuns and Nones meetings—he isn't much interested in spiritual conversation with Catholic sisters. But we do still gather each month with our Interfaith Supper Club from Calvary. We sit elbow-to-elbow around picnic tables, asking other couples questions about values and celebrating holidays and raising kids in mixed-faith homes. (The jury is still out on Bible camp.)

I am not spiritually single. None of us is. But it is our continued struggle to love and bless one another, doubters and believers, nuns and nones, outsiders and insiders alike, that will carry the charism forward.

ACKNOWLEDGMENTS

*T*here are many ordinary saints who helped make this book possible.

First, to the Visitation Sisters of North Minneapolis—Brenda, Katherine, Karen, Mary Frances, Mary Margaret, Mary Paula, Mary Virginia, and Suzanne—thank you for inviting me into your lives and for loving your neighbors so well. Thank you for your trust and for providing me with a room to write in on the third floor of the monastery. What a gift. Special thanks to Sisters Brenda and Katherine for reading an early draft of this manuscript and for your feedback; any errors in my Catholic theology or otherwise are mine alone. I am grateful to the Visitation Companions, particularly Jody Johnson who answered many of my questions about Salesian spirituality. Thank you to Brian Mogren for opening up the Saint Jane House to me for several writing retreats.

Calvary Baptist Church, you have my heart. Pastors Jeff and Amy, I am grateful for how you welcome all kinds of families on Sunday mornings. Thank you especially to the Interfaith Supper Club for your friendship: Angie and Chris, Julie and Pete, Savannah and Jessie, and our newest additions, Emily and Nate. I really do love our church.

I am grateful every day I get to work for the Collegeville Institute. Thank you to my colleagues, particularly Don

Ottenhoff, Laura Fanucci, and Susan Sink, for encouraging me to make my own writing a priority. Lauren F. Winner introduced me to the craft of spiritual memoir, and this book is much improved thanks to her helpful edits. I am indebted to Timothy Jones, Erin S. Lane, and Heidi Neumark for reading a terrible first draft of this book during the summer of 2019. Thank you for wading through the muck and finding the gems. Also, my gratitude to past Collegeville Institute writing teachers Mary Potter and Jonathan Wilson-Hartgrove for investing in me.

IVP has been an absolute joy to work with. You all are wonderful humans who reflect God's good grace. Thank you in particular to Ethan McCarthy for your astute edits and thoughtful questions, to Lori Neff for your good humor and marketing prowess, and to art director David Fassett for the gorgeous cover design. My thanks also to Rebecca Gill, Krista Clayton, Tara Burns, and countless others who worked behind the scenes. I am grateful to Katelyn Beaty for believing in this book and for pushing me to write the proposal in the first place. Also, my deep gratitude to artist Gracie Morbitzer for her gorgeous paintings and for granting me permission to use them in this book.

I would never have written this book without the support from my writing communities. Jessica Goudeau, Kelley Nikondeha, D. L. Mayfield, Amy Peterson, and Christiana Peterson, thank you for being there for every step along the journey. Special thanks to writers in my local community who have cheered me on over the years, especially Claire DeBerg and Kelsey Maddox. Ellie Roscher coached me during the

home stretch when I didn't think I could finish the book—thank you for all the encouraging texts and phone calls. I am grateful to the Loft Literary Center writing teachers, especially Kate St. Vincent Vogl. A special thank you to Mary Kenagy Mitchell at *Image Journal* and Andrea Palpant Dilley at *Christianity Today* for editing and publishing my first essays about mixed-faith marriage—you gave me the confidence that I could write this story well

To the Louisville Institute: thank you for entrusting me with a 2019 Pastoral Study Grant, and to Katie Gordon and Ellie Hutchison Cervantes for partnering with me. To the Catholic sisters I have met through Nuns and Nones in the Twin Cities, Sisters Jill and Stephanie in particular, thank you for your generous conversation and companionship.

A special thank you to Caroline for allowing me to tell part of your sacred story. I hope you write your own book someday.

Thank you to our supportive families, especially our parents Jim and Deb, John and Anita. You love us and our kids so well. Laurie, Sarah, Abram, Bethany, Jonathan, Benjamin, Kirsten, and Lydia—I hit the sibling jackpot. To all our grandparents and extended family in North Carolina and beyond, thank you.

Finally, to Eliza and Rowan: may you know the love of God all the days of your life. Being your mom is the best job I've ever had.

And to Josh: I admire your honest struggle, integrity, and pursuit of truth. Thank you for encouraging me to tell our story, for reading drafts of this book, and for taking the kids on countless bike rides so I could finish writing it. I love you.

NOTES

1. THE FALLOUT

5   *As I take my spade in hand*: Kathleen Norris, *The Cloister Walk* (New York: Riverhead, 1996), 32.

10   *If you're not aligned*: Scott Kedersha, quoted in FamilyLife (@FamilyLife-Today), Twitter, July 15, 2019, 9:50 a.m., https://twitter.com/FamilyLife Today/status/1150779578799067136.

     Most generational cohorts: Michael Lipka, "Millennials Increasingly Are Driving Growth of 'Nones,'" Pew Research Center, May 12, 2015, www .pewresearch.org/fact-tank/2015/05/12/millennials-increasingly-are -driving-growth-of-nones/.

11   *Divorce statistics of interfaith marriages*: Naomi Schaefer Riley, *'Til Faith Do Us Part: How Interfaith Marriage Is Transforming America* (New York: Oxford University Press, 2013), 121.

6. NEW MONASTICISM

35   *School(s) for Conversion: 12 Marks of a New Monasticism*, The Rutba House, ed. (Eugene, OR: Cascade, 2005).

39   *Demonstration plot for the kingdom*: "Brief History," Koinonia Farm, accessed February 13, 2020, www.koinoniafarm.org/brief-history/.

7. READING APOCALYPTIC SCRIPTURES, AS A FAMILY

46   *Advent guide:* Tsh Oxenrider, "A Simple Advent Guide," https://tshoxenreider .com/shop/advent/.

9. MOSCOW SPIRITUALITY

57   *Moscow had only six minutes*: Charles Maynes, "Moscow Sees Only 6 Minutes of Sunlight During All of December," *All Things Considered*, January 18, 2018, https://www.npr.org/2018/01/18/578956832/moscow -sees-only-6-minutes-of-sunlight-during-all-of-december.

10. GOOD INTENTIONS

64   *I offer you*: Francis de Sales, *St. Francis de Sales: Selected Letters*, ed. and with an introduction by Elisabeth Stopp, 2nd ed. (Stella Niagara, NY: DeSales Resource Center, 2011), 152.

12. MY MYSTICAL SISTERS, THE SAINTS

77   *Robert Ellsberg's book*: Robert Ellsberg, *Blessed Among All Women: Women Saints, Prophets, and Witnesses for Our Time* (New York: Crossroad, 2007), 18.

78   *story of each holy person*: Ellsberg, *Blessed Among All Women*, 18.

13. JANUARY 23: SAINT JANE

79 *If I ever become a Saint*: Mother Teresa, *Come Be My Light: The Private Writings of the "Saint of Calcutta,"* ed. Brian Kolodiejchuk (New York: Image, 2009), 230.

82 *De Paul wrote*: Robert Ellsberg, *Blessed Among All Women: Women Saints, Prophets, and Witnesses for Our Time* (New York: Crossroad, 2007), 39.

83 *Saint Francis de Sales once wrote*: Saint Francis de Sales, Jane de Chantal, *Francis de Sales, Jane de Chantal: Letters of Spiritual Direction, Classics of Western Spirituality*, ed. Wendy M. Wright and Joseph F. Power, trans. Péronne Marie Thibert (Mahwah, NJ: Paulist Press, 1988), 34.

in the choices they made: Ellsberg, *Blessed Among All Women*, 16.

14. DISCERNING THE WAY YOU SHOULD GO

90 *between God's two wills*: Sister Katherine, "Discernment: What Francis de Sales Calls the 'Two Wills of God' Talk," Visitation Monastery of Minneapolis, November 1, 2010, www.visitationmonasteryminneapolis .org/2010/11/living-between-the-two-wills-of-god-st-francis-de-sales -speaks-through-sister-katherine/.

15. THE LITTLE VIRTUES

94 *nun instructing teenage women*: Elsa Thompson Hofmeister, *Extraordinary Ordinary Lives: Vocation Stories of Minnesota Visitation Sisters* (Willow River, MN: James Monroe, 2009).

17. RELINQUISHMENT

105 *Merriam-Webster*, s.v. "relinquish (*v. tr.*)," accessed March 31, 2020, www .merriam-webster.com/dictionary/relinquish.

108 *more nuns over the age of ninety*: Erick Berrelleaz, Mary L. Gautier, and Mark M. Gray, "Population Trends Among Religious Institutes of Women," *Center for Applied Research in the Apostolate Special Report*, Fall 2014. https://cara.georgetown.edu/wp-content/uploads/2018/06 /Women_Religious_Fall2014_FINAL.pdf.

112 *"rightsizing" more than "downsizing"*: Dan Stockman, "Religious Communities Face Changes, Plan to Retain Missions and Preserve History," *Global Sisters Report*, June 2, 2016, www.globalsistersreport.org/news /trends/religious-communities-face-changes-plan-retain-missions-and -preserve-history-40136.

It's like a secret spiral: Richard Rohr, "The Universal Pattern: Loss and Renewal," Center for Action and Contemplation, April 24, 2017, https:// cac.org/universal-pattern-loss-renewal-2017-04-24.

19. HOLY WEEK

120 *self-differentiation:* Richard Niolon, "Bowenian Family Therapy," Psych-Page, accessed March 31, 2020, www.psychpage.com/learning/library/counseling/bowen.html#Z3.

121 *Wash not just my feet:* John 13:9.

What if Judas: Rachelle Linner, "Tonight—Holy Thursday," *Give Us This Day,* 8, no. 3 (March 2018): 341.

123 *To take up our cross:* Francis de Sales, *Every Day with Saint Francis de Sales,* comp. Augustine Archenti and Arnold Pedrini, trans. W. L. Cornell, ed. Francis J. Klauder, "Sermons 2, Oeuvres 9" (New Rochelle, NY: Salesiana Publishers, 1985), 18.

20. SPIRITUAL WEATHER REPORT

129 *Weather fluctuations:* Saint Francis de Sales quoted in, Lewis S. Fiorelli, *Inspired Common Sense: Seven Fundamental Themes of Salesian Spirituality* (Stella Niagara, NY: DeSales Resource Center, 2012), 43-44.

132 *not waste our energy:* Saint Francis de Sales, *Selected Letters* trans. Elisabeth Stopp, 2nd ed. (Stella Niagara, NY: DeSales Resource Center, 2011), 61.

21. MAY 3: ELISABETH LESEUR

133 *found herself married:* Wendy Wright, preface to Janet K. Ruffing, *Elisabeth Leseur: Selected Writings,* Classics of Western Spirituality (Mahwah, NJ: Paulist Press, 2005), 1.

135 *approach the abyss:* Felix Leseur, "In Memoriam" in Elisabeth Leseur, *The Secret Diary of Elisabeth Leseur: The Woman Whose Goodness Changed Her Husband from Atheist to Priest* (Manchester, NY: Sophia Institute Press, 2002), xxiii.

commitment to silence: Janet K. Ruffing, "Elizabeth Leseur: A Strangely Forgotten Modern Saint," in *Lay Sanctity, Medieval and Modern,* ed. Ann W. Astell (Notre Dame, IN: University of Notre Dame Press, 2000), 120.

136 *arguments or discussion was futile:* Ruffing, "Elizabeth Leseur," 120.

in order to surrender: Ruffing, "Elizabeth Leseur," 123.

22. ON VOWS

142 *I want you:* Elsa Thompson Hofmeister, *Extraordinary Ordinary Lives: Vocation Stories of Minnesota Visitation Sisters* (Willow River, MN: James Monroe, 2009), 278.

144 *public witness to Gospel values:* Joan Chittister, *Fire in These Ashes* (Franklin, WI: Sheed & Ward, 1995), 100.

147 *The very nature of marriage:* Kathleen Norris, *Acedia and Me* (New York: Riverhead Books, 2008), 180.

147   *What the world needs now*: Joan Chittister, *The Fire in These Ashes: A Spirituality of Contemporary Religious Life* (Franklin, WI: Sheed and Ward, 1995), 102.

148   *makes growth possible*: Chittister, *Fire in These Ashes*, 83.

24. LIFE TOGETHER

162   *my friend Kendra wrote*: Kendra Langdon Juskus, www.instagram.com /slowpoetklj

25. JUNE 8: SAINT MARGARET MARY

170   *The Gifts of Imperfection: Let Go of Who You Think You're Supposed to Be and Embrace Who You Are*, Brené Brown (Center City, MN: Hazelden, 2010), 87.

26. COMMON GRACE

173   *The life of mortals*: Psalm 103:15-16.

27. "I THINK I LOVE GOD"

176   *It rises and falls*: Flannery O'Connor, *The Habit of Being: Letters of Flannery O'Connor*, ed. Sally Fitzgerald (New York: Farrar, Straus and Giroux, 1979), 452.

29. NUNS' PICNIC

188   *The word* obey: Kathleen Norris, *Acedia and Me* (New York: Riverhead Books, 2008), 183.

190   *marriage "serves us best"*: Wendell Berry, *Standing by Words* (Berkeley, CA: Counterpoint, 1983), 97.

32. NOVEMBER 2: ALL SOULS' DAY

211   *intercession of saints and angels*: David Lamb, "The Communion of Saints: Dead or Alive in Christ?" Evangelical Catholic Apologetics, accessed February 27, 2020, http://www.biblicalcatholic.com/apologetics/a96.htm.
      dead can accompany us: Robert J. Carlson, "Praying for Those Who Have Died Is a Spiritual Work of Mercy," Catholic News Agency, August 11, 2011, https://www.catholicnewsagency.com/column/praying-for-those-who -have-died-is-a-spiritual-work-of-mercy-1739.

34. FEBRUARY 8: MORNING PRAYER

226   *I wear the image:* This paragraph and the two that follow are lightly adapted from Stina Kielsmeier-Cook, "Evangelists of Love: Billy Graham and Francis de Sales," Bearings Online, February 23, 2018, https:// collegevilleinstitute.org/bearings/evangelists-of-love.

227   *Blessed are the agnostics*: I can't find the verbatim transcript of her talk from the 2016 Festival of Faith and Writing, but this is taken from her book: Nadia Bolz-Weber, *Accidental Saints: Finding God in All the Wrong People* (New York: Convergent Books, 2015), 184-85.